AMUSEMENT PARKS
of Virginia, Maryland, and Delaware

JIM FUTRELL

STACKPOLE
BOOKS

Published by
STACKPOLE BOOKS
5067 Ritter Road
Mechanicsburg, PA 17055
www.stackpolebooks.com

Printed in the United States of America

10 9 8 7 6 5 4 3 2 1

FIRST EDITION

Design by Beth Oberholtzer
Cover design by Wendy Reynolds

Library of Congress Cataloging-in-Publication Data

Futrell, Jim.
    Amusement parks of Virginia, Maryland, and Delaware / Jim Futrell.
    – 1st ed.
        p.   cm.
    Includes bibliographical references and index.
    ISBN-13: 978-0-8117-3475-2 (pbk.)
    ISBN-10: 0-8117-3475-7 (pbk.)
    1. Amusement parks.   2. Amusement parks–Delaware–Guidebooks.
3. Amusement parks–Maryland–Guidebooks.   4. Amusement parks–
Virginia–Guidebooks.   I. Title.

GV1853.2.F88   2008
791.06'80975–dc22
                                                        2007025990

CONTENTS

FOREWORD

FROM FERRIS WHEELS TO ROLLER COASTERS TO TUNNELS OF LOVE, EVERY-
body in this business has a favorite amusement park memory. When Jim
Futrell first asked me to write the foreword for this book, I began to con-
template my life in this business and to think of my favorite memories
through the years. I've been in the amusement park business for forty-
seven years and have traveled the world many times over, yet my favorite
memories are those spent in Virginia in the late 1970s and early 1980s
at Kings Dominion theme park. Even though our industry has grown and
matured, and has met the challenges that come with technology and
changing demographics, one thing remains certain. People of all ages
simply want to have fun.

The Mid-Atlantic region—or more specifically the Chesapeake Bay
area of Virginia, Maryland, and Delaware—is distinguished by its strong
roots in amusement park history. This is evident when one remembers
the parks that thrived in that region during the industry's glory days,
such as Carlin's Amusement Park, Enchanted Forest, River View Park,
Seaside Park, Story Book Land, and Luna Park. For nearly 130 years,
many amusement park aficionados have made their memories at amusement parks in Virginia, Maryland, and Delaware.

Even though those amusement parks have now closed, other vintage
parks remain and newer, world-class theme parks abound. As you journey through the beautiful Chesapeake Bay area—first through the pages
of this book and then I hope in person—it is my desire that you will enjoy
and appreciate the distinctive attractions that offer historical significance as well as take advantage of the region's world-class theme parks.

The tristate region consisting of Virginia, Maryland, and Delaware contains it all—a bit of nostalgia, a bit of old-fashioned midway charm, and a bit of high-tech thrill. And, family fun is at the core of everything. Year after year, these three states proudly offer world-class and long-established entertainment that appeals to all ages.

If you are looking for time-honored and old-fashioned forms of family entertainment, this region has it. In Delaware, you can experience Funland, an amusement center family-owned-and-operated since 1939. Your little ones will also love Jolly Roger Amusement Park in Maryland as they drive go-carts, climb a rock wall, or play miniature golf.

If nostalgia suits your fancy, you must cruise down Ocean City, Maryland's Coastal Highway strip during the popular summer season. Along this drive, one cannot escape the image of a quintessential American beach resort. From a single inlet extends the nearly three-mile, amusement-filled boardwalk, which dates back to the early twentieth century. Funnel cakes, candy apples, ice cream, arcade games, and rides at classic locations such as Trimper's Rides or Jolly Roger at the Pier give you the chance to feel like a kid again and relive childhood memories. While in Maryland, don't forget to stop at Frontier Town. This jewel of an attraction has been stuck in time for more than forty years. It was a gem in 1959 and still is today. The cowboys and outlaws try hard to make you think you're in the Old West, through train rides, pony rides, saloon shows, bank holdups, and gunfights.

Speaking of theme parks, no mention of amusement park history is complete without also discussing the incredible way that theme parks have evolved from humble roots. What once began as pleasure gardens in Europe in the eighteenth century soon spread to America in the late nineteenth century. Amusement parks in the golden era were prevalent until the 1920s, and were the precursors to the modern-day theme park era. Virginia, Maryland, and Delaware offer several traditional, yet classic, amusement facilities that you will gain a new appreciation for after reading this book. At the same time, however, these three states also boast three of the best modern-day theme parks, where rides, shows, and attractions are abundant among distinctively themed areas.

Virginia, with its European roots, is home to Busch Gardens Europe. This theme park has been voted the world's Most Beautiful Theme Park every year since 1991 and is a fixture among the world's Favorite Theme Parks in the annual National Amusement Park Historical Association members' survey. Its European setting is distinctively exhibited in its nine organized "hamlets" themed after six prominent European countries.

Kings Dominion is also located in Virginia. Much has changed at Kings Dominion since those early days when I was there in the '70s. What hasn't changed, though, is Kings Dominion's emphasis on family fun and world-class entertainment. Throughout its seven themed areas, and its Water-Works water park, this theme park offers world-class rides and attractions. Maryland is home to Six Flags America in Prince George's County. This park has roots dating back to 1974. Its seven themed areas offer everything from world-class roller coasters Batwing and Superman, to the family-oriented Tea Cups and carousel.

As you will see when reading this book, the amusement attractions in the Mid-Atlantic region states of Virginia, Maryland, and Delaware are unique. Their roots in the amusement park business are solid. A visit to the Mid-Atlantic region is not complete without a visit to at least one of the diverse amusement attractions offered by this soothing and charming part of America. I have mentioned only a few of the myriad of attractions available. This book by Jim Futrell, on the other hand, offers a unique and telling look at Virginia, Maryland, and Delaware—their character as well as their profound significance in the amusement park business both past and present. I am deeply honored to have been asked to share this foreword with you.

Whether you seek thrills, nostalgia, world-class roller coasters, water attractions, picturesque seaside amusement settings, or old-fashioned family fun parks, you will find it in the quaint Chesapeake Bay area. And when you do, I know you will make your own amusement park memory that will, like mine, last a lifetime.

Dennis Spiegel
President
International Theme Park Services, Inc.

ACKNOWLEDGMENTS

NO BOOK IS POSSIBLE WITHOUT THE SUPPORT OF NUMEROUS INDIVIDUALS. This one is no different. From the amusement parks themselves to their employees to the support and encouragement provided by family, friends, and coworkers, this book was the result of more than my efforts. Were it not for the generosity of the following people, this book would not have been possible.

Thanks would have to start with Kyle Weaver of Stackpole Books, who came up with the idea for a series of books profiling America's amusement parks. Thanks also have to go to his assistant Brett Keener for all of his hard work.

The amusement parks in Virginia, Maryland, and Delaware were very cooperative and I am certainly grateful for all of their assistance: Granville Trimper, Brooks Trimper, and Johnnie Jett at Trimper's Rides and Amusements; Stephen Pastusak at Bayshore Development, owner of Jolly Roger at the Pier and Jolly Roger Amusement Park; Al Fasnacht at Funland, Rehoboth Beach, Delaware; Nelson, Todd, and Fran Kennedy at Frontier Town; Tom and Sara Kuhn at Funland, McHenry, Maryland; Ed Kuhlman and Susie Storey at Kings Dominion; Karin Korpowski at Six Flags America; Cindy Sarko at Busch Gardens Europe; Steve Hoffman at Baja Amusements; Kevin Bryan at Motor World; Robert Miller at Go-Karts Plus; Bruce Mimran at Virginia Beach Amusement Park; Joan Passala and Ernie DeCarlo at Blue Diamond Park; and Larry Stottlemyer at Adventure Park USA.

I would also like to thank Dennis Spiegel for writing the foreword and sharing his memories of Kings Dominion and Ed Householder for his help in formatting the pictures.

Thanks are also due my family and friends for all of their support during the two-year process of making this book a reality. In particular, I would like to recognize Dave, Terry, and David Hahner for their help in choosing the pictures.

Four people deserve my special gratitude for making this book a reality—my wife and best friend Marlowe, and our sons Jimmy, Christopher, and Matthew. They share and appreciate my passion for amusement parks and I hope they will always remember the good times we had exploring the delightful variety of amusement parks in Virginia, Maryland, and Delaware.

Finally I would like to give a special thank-you to my parents, Jim and Joanne Futrell. When I was a young kid just starting to discover my amusement park passion, they never dismissed my interest but went out of their way to encourage and support it. They will always have a special place in my heart for that.

INTRODUCTION

THERE IS A WORLD OF MEMORIES AWAITING YOU AT THE AMUSEMENT parks in Virginia, Maryland, and Delaware. This region is defined by its relationship with the Atlantic Ocean, its history, the large cities that run along the Interstate 95 corridor, and the incredible diversity of topography. Rolling mountains, pristine beaches, and miles of rivers large and small are all present in this area. In addition, the area is home to three action-packed boardwalks: Rehoboth Beach, Ocean City, and Virginia Beach, each with its own personality.

With this geographical diversity, it is not surprising that the area is also defined by an amazing variety of amusement parks to enjoy. The three large world-class theme parks—Busch Gardens Europe, Kings Dominion, and Six Flags America—stand out in a category by themselves, offering cutting-edge thrill rides, world-class roller coasters and attractions, and enough activities to fill at least one full day. But you are cheating yourself if you stop there.

Trimper's Rides and Amusements in the resort community of Ocean City is the oldest seaside amusement park in the country and a treasure trove of historic rides including one of the most magnificent carousels found anywhere. Nearby, Jolly Roger at the Pier is a classic amusement pier complete with a giant Ferris wheel, while Jolly Roger Park, its sister facility, offers a full day of activities with its amusement park, water park, and go-cart park. Funland in Rehoboth Beach has one of the country's finest traditional dark rides and some of the industry's lowest prices, while Frontier Town represents one of the last examples of a staple of the family vacation in the 1950s and 1960s—the themed roadside attraction. If go-carts are your speed, some of the top go-cart parks in the country can be found at Baja Amusements and Motor World. The new breed of amusement park known as family entertainment centers is well represented by two award-winning facilities—Go-Karts Plus and Adventure Park USA. Meanwhile, Virginia Beach Amusement Park and Blue Diamond Park are two of the country's newest, albeit most traditional, facilities.

What is most fascinating about these places is that no matter how large or small, how old or new, or whether they are owned by a family or a large corporation, they each have a unique story of how they came into existence and grew to their present size. I have tried to convey those stories so that you can truly appreciate each park's personality when you visit.

But before you venture out, here are a few general tips to make your day more enjoyable:

- *Check the website.* Most parks have websites that provide up-to-date information. Always check right before your visit to confirm hours and prices. You can also check for special events and promotions. Many have discount coupons or opportunities to purchase reduced price tickets.

- *Dress comfortably.* Make sure you wear comfortable shoes that are broken in. Also wear cool, loose-fitting clothes (but not too loose, they might get caught on something) and bring a jacket and a rain poncho, just in case.

- *Pack lightly.* You're going to be walking around all day, so don't weigh yourself down with a lot of stuff. Many parks have lockers where you can store things you might need during the day.

- *Eat a good breakfast.* Arriving at the park hungry means that you might waste time that could otherwise be spent riding. Don't stuff yourself with greasy food, however. It doesn't mix well with rides.

- *Arrive early.* Typically the best time of day at an amusement park is the first hour that it is open, before the bulk of the people show up. This is often the time to ride some of the big rides.

- *Hit the big rides first.* While most visitors tend to rush to the big rides first, the lines will only increase as the day wears on, although they usually grow shorter in the evening, when the roller coasters tend to be running faster. Try to avoid the big rides between noon and 5 P.M.

- *Follow the rules.* All parks have certain rules and regulations and set height limits for certain rides and attractions. A great deal of thought has gone into developing these limits and they are there to protect you. Please respect them.

Finally, one of the great things about amusement parks is that they are constantly evolving and changing. Although every effort had been made to ensure the accuracy of the book, some changes may have occurred.

A History of the Amusement Park Industry

HUMAN BEINGS ARE, BY NATURE, SOCIAL CREATURES. SINCE THE BEGIN-ning of time, people have sought ways to come together and escape the pressures of everyday life. As humankind started to settle in villages, festivals and celebrations became popular ways for the community to relax. As villages grew into cities, parcels of land were set aside as sort of a permanent festival. In Europe, these places were known as pleasure gardens.

In the sixteenth and seventeenth centuries, pleasure gardens sprang up on the outskirts of major cities. At a time when Europe's cities were crowded, dirty, disease-ridden places, these pleasure gardens provided a welcome respite. In many ways, they were similar to today's amusement parks, offering landscaped gardens, live entertainment, fireworks, dancing, games, and even primitive amusement rides, including the fore-runners of today's merry-go-rounds, Ferris wheels, and roller coasters.

Pleasure gardens remained extremely popular until the late eigh-teenth century, when political unrest and urban sprawl caused a decline that lasted until the middle of the next century. Though most of the pleasure gardens are now faded memories, two still exist. Dyrehavs Bakken, which opened in 1583 outside Copenhagen, Denmark, is the world's old-est operating amusement park; and the Prater in Vienna, which got its start in 1766 when the emperor turned a portion of his private hunting preserve over to public amusement, is now a beloved Viennese tradition.

1

Belleville Mountains in Paris was an example of the primitive roller coaster rides that were popular at European pleasure gardens in the early 1800s.

Coming to America

As the pleasure garden was dying out in Europe, a new nation, the United States, was growing into a world power. Immigrants flocking to cities such as New York, Philadelphia, and Boston clamored for recreation. Entrepreneurs responded by developing picnic groves and beer gardens throughout America.

Jones Woods, widely accepted as America's first large amusement resort, opened along the East River in New York in the early 1800s. Its attractions included bowling, billiards, gymnasium equipment, a shooting gallery, donkey rides, music, dancing, and a beer garden. The popularity of Jones Woods was short-lived, however, as the rapid growth of Manhattan overtook the resort in the 1860s.

The continuing demand for amusement in New York was soon answered on a peninsula in Brooklyn known as Coney Island, named for the coneys, or wild rabbits, that inhabited the area. The seaside location provided a cool getaway in the hot summer months, and in 1829, a hotel catering to visitors appeared on the sands. By the early 1850s, pavilions offering bathing, dining, and dancing were being constructed at Coney Island. Around 1875, a railroad to the resort was completed, and the destination's popularity quickly increased. Entrepreneurs responded by opening cabarets, vaudeville theaters, fortune-telling booths, games, and rides such as small carousels. Here, in 1867, a creative restaurateur named Charles Feltman invented the hot dog. The resort's first major amusement device opened in 1877, when the Iron Tower was installed. This 300-foot-tall observation tower was relocated from the 1876 Philadelphia Centennial Exposition, where it was known as the Sawyer Observatory. Just seven years later, in 1884, the modern roller coaster was invented when LaMarcus Thompson built the Switchback Railway along the seashore. Throughout its history, however, Coney Island was never an amusement park, but a neighborhood in Brooklyn that featured a collection of amusements, including several independent amusement parks.

Early amusement resort growth was not confined to New York. In 1846, large crowds gathered at a family farm in Bristol, Connecticut, to view a failed science experiment. The size of the crowd convinced the farm's owner, Gad Norton, that there was a big need for a recreational gathering place in central Connecticut. Norton converted his farm into an amusement resort called Lake Compounce, where people could enjoy picnicking, boating in the lake, listening to band concerts, and dancing. Today Lake Compounce continues as the oldest operating amusement park in the United States. Another early amusement resort, called Rocky Point Park, opened nearby in Warwick, Rhode Island, in 1847. This seaside resort continued to operate until 1995.

In the years following the Civil War, the personality of the country changed as America's cities became increasingly congested and industrialized. Farmers flocked to the cities to find jobs in the new factories. The growing congestion encouraged many to seek out recreation away from the cities. Many amusement resorts opened along the ocean shore or by a lake, where people could find a cool getaway in the hot summer. But the primary engine for the development of the amusement park in America was the trolley company.

In the wake of the opening of the first practical electric-powered street rail line in Richmond in 1888, hundreds of trolley lines popped up around the country almost overnight. At that time, utility companies charged the trolley companies a flat fee for the use of their electricity. The transportation companies looked for a way to stimulate weekend ridership to make the most of their investment. Opening amusement resorts provided the ideal solution. Typically built at the end of the trolley lines, these resorts initially were simple operations consisting of picnic facilities, dance halls, restaurants, games, and a few amusement rides. These parks were immediately successful and soon opened across America.

Celoron Park in New York was typical of the hundreds of trolley parks that opened throughout the United States in the late nineteenth and early twentieth centuries.

Becoming an American Institution

The amusement park became an institution in the wake of the 1893 World's Columbian Exposition in Chicago. This world's fair introduced the Ferris wheel and the amusement midway to the world. The midway, essentially a wide walkway lined with an array of rides and concessions, was a huge success and set the precedent for amusement park design for the next sixty years. The following year, Capt. Paul Boyton borrowed the midway concept and opened the world's first modern amusement park, Paul Boyton's Water Chutes, on Chicago's South Side. Boyton was a colorful figure who served in the Union navy during the Civil War and fought in the Franco-Prussian War. In 1874, he stowed away on an ocean liner with the intent of jumping overboard 200 miles out to sea to test an "unsinkable" rubber lifesaving suit. He was apprehended but was eventually permitted by the captain to jump overboard 30 miles off the coast of Ireland. Boyton safely made it to land, achieving international fame. He followed that accomplishment by becoming the first person to swim the English Channel. In 1888, he settled in Chicago, where he started an aquatic circus and raised sea lions in Lake Michigan. Soon he came across a Shoot the Chutes water ride in Rock Island, Illinois, where it had been invented in 1889. Boyton was intrigued by the simple ride, in which a boat traveled down an inclined plane into a body of water. This was the first major water-based amusement ride and the forerunner of today's log flumes and splashdown rides. Boyton purchased the rights to the Shoot the Chutes and tested it in London in 1893 before setting it up in Chicago as the centerpiece of his new park.

Unlike the primitive trolley parks, which were just starting to come into their own, Boyton's Water Chutes was the first amusement park to charge admission and use rides as its main draw, rather than picnic facilities or a natural feature such as a beach or a lake. Patrons from all over Chicago flocked to Captain Boyton's operation to ride the 60-foot-tall Water Chutes. More than five hundred thousand people showed up in that first season alone. Boyton's park relocated to a larger site in 1896, but it closed in 1908, eclipsed by larger and more modern facilities. The success of his Chicago park, however, inspired him to open a similar facility, Sea Lion Park, at the fledgling Coney Island resort in New York in 1895. The park featured not only a water chute ride, but also the Flip Flap, one of the first looping roller coasters, and a sea lion show that foreshadowed those at today's theme parks.

Sea Lion Park was Coney Island's first true amusement park—a collection of rides and shows in a fenced area to which patrons paid admission. With the opening of Sea Lion Park, Coney Island became the center of the amusement universe. Entrepreneurs from all over flocked to develop new rides and attractions for the masses. George Tilyou, a successful Coney Island restaurant operator, opened Steeplechase Park in 1897. The park, with its well-manicured gardens, took amusement to a whole new level. Soon the park became internationally renowned for its signature Steeplechase ride, which allowed patrons to experience the thrills of a horse race by riding wooden horses along eight parallel, undulating tracks.

The success of Steeplechase Park hurt business at Sea Lion Park, and in 1902, Boyton sold the struggling operation to businessmen Frederick Thompson and Elmer Dundy. The two men found fame at the Pan American Exposition in Buffalo in 1901, when they introduced their successful Trip to the Moon, one of the first simulator attractions. After moving it to Steeplechase Park, where they operated it for the 1902 season, they wanted to set out on their own. The result of this ambition was Luna Park, reportedly named after Dundy's sister. Described in advertisements as "an electric Eden unlike anything that had ever been built before," it was characterized by its fanciful "Arabian Nights" style of architecture outlined by 250,000 electric lights. At a time when electrical lighting was rare in most houses, Luna Park created a sensation, attracting over forty thousand patrons at its opening in May 1903.

Luna Park represented a new genre of amusement park known as the exposition park, which looked to the Chicago world's fair for inspiration.

These parks featured elaborate buildings with fanciful designs outlined with thousands of electric lights. There were attractions that were considered very complex for their time, such as re-creations of famous disasters, scaled-down replicas of distant lands, and displays of prematurely born infants being cared for with technology so advanced that even hospitals had yet to install it. Unlike the more pastoral trolley parks, exposition parks tended to be raucous, packed with attractions, and located close to urban centers.

Among the more famous exposition parks were White City in Chicago (opened in 1905); Luna Park in Pittsburgh (1905); Luna Park in Cleveland (1905); and Wonderland near Boston (1906). While most larger cities featured an exposition park, the phenomenon was largely short-lived because of high overhead and the high cost of the new attractions they added. One, however, remains in operation: Lakeside Park in Denver, which opened as White City in 1908 and still features its elaborate Tower of Jewels.

Perhaps the grandest exposition park of them all was Dreamland, which opened across the street from Coney Island's Luna Park in 1904. Dreamland tried to top Luna Park in every respect. At the center of the park was a 375-foot-tall tower; the buildings were outlined with a million electric lights, and the entire place was adorned with elaborate facades, fountains, pools, and floral displays. Among the attractions

With its elaborate architecture, Luna Park at Coney Island in New York created a whole new genre of amusement park when it opened in 1903.

were Lilliputia, a complete city populated by 300 little people, and the huge Fighting the Flames show, which claimed to have a cast of 4,000. With the opening of Dreamland, Coney Island was at its zenith, with three immense amusement parks and dozens of individual concessions catering to the millions that flocked there. Steeplechase's Tilyou was quoted as stating, "If Paris is France, then Coney Island between May and September is the world."

Even a fire at Steeplechase Park in 1907 that burned the park and a large portion of the surrounding neighborhood to the ground failed to put a damper on things. After charging customers ten cents a head to view the "burning ruins," owner George Tilyou immediately rebuilt the park bigger and better than ever. The Steeplechase ride remained and encircled the Pavilion of Fun, a 5-acre building featuring rides and fun house devices.

Unfortunately, fire became a constant nemesis of Coney Island, with twenty major conflagrations striking the resort area through its history. The largest completely destroyed Dreamland and fifty other businesses just after the start of the 1911 season. Never as successful as Luna Park or Steeplechase, Dreamland was underinsured and as a result, was not rebuilt, although other amusement attractions soon moved in on the ruins to take Dreamland's place. The destruction of Dreamland signified the beginning of Coney Island's slow decline, however. The following year, Luna Park went bankrupt, but it managed to hold on until 1944, when it too was done in by fire. Steeplechase closed in 1964 and sat abandoned for two years before being demolished. Into the 1980s, many of Coney Island's remaining landmarks succumbed—the once great restaurants and bathhouses, and three of its greatest roller coasters: the Bobsled in 1974, the Tornado in 1977, and the Thunderbolt in 1982. Although only a fraction of its original size, Coney Island has hung on, and it is enjoying a renewed appreciation with its surviving vintage attractions, such as the 1920 Wonder Wheel and the 1927 vintage Cyclone roller coaster, both now listed as national landmarks. The rebounding area has even caught the attention of several major developers who have announced ambitious plans to bring new development to the neighborhood.

The success of Coney Island during the early part of the twentieth century helped spread the amusement park industry throughout the country. Trolley companies, breweries, and entrepreneurs opened parks by the hundreds. The number of operating parks grew from approximately 250 in 1899 to nearly 700 in 1905. By 1919, more than 1,500 amusement parks were in operation in the United States. In 1913, *World's Work* magazine described the growth as "a hysteria of parks followed by a panic." *Billboard* magazine sounded a cautionary message in 1909: "The great profits made by some of the park men produce a mania for park building, which can well be compared to some of the booms in mining camps. Men from almost all professions of life flocked to this endeavor, and without knowledge or particular ability in this line endeavored to build parks." Soon every major city had at least one park.

Amusement parks during this time had a much different personality than they do today. A review of the industry by *Billboard* magazine in 1905 summed up the keys to a successful attraction as "plenty of shade, attractive landscaping, sufficient transportation, first class attractions (live entertainment) and a variety of good up to date privileges," as rides and concessions were then known. Rides were almost an afterthought in the article and only mentioned after an in-depth discussion of the importance of a summer theater presenting summer stock, vaudeville, and concerts, which it considered to be the heart of the park. But that personality would soon change.

The Golden Age

With amusement parks opening at such a rapid pace in the early twentieth century, patrons were looking for more thrilling attractions, and soon a whole new industry sprang up to fulfill this need. The William F. Mangels Company was founded at Coney Island in 1890 and in 1914 introduced the whip, one of the first mass-produced rides. The Eli Bridge Company started operations in 1900 and to this day continues to manufacture the Ferris wheels that are a midway staple. The Philadelphia Toboggan Company, one of the largest manufacturers of roller coasters and carousels, started making rides in 1904 and thrives today making trains for wooden roller coasters. In 1912, the Dayton Fun House Company was formed. This company was the forerunner to National Amusement Devices and, later, International Amusement Devices, one of the largest and most prolific builders of amusement rides before its demise in the mid-1980s. The Dodgem Corporation opened in 1919 in Salisbury Beach, Massachusetts, introducing bumper cars to amusement parks.

In the competition to sell the most rides, innovation was the watchword of the era. Riverview Park in Chicago built a roller coaster called the Potsdam Railway in 1908, in which the cars were suspended beneath the track rather than riding above it. In 1912, John Miller, the most prolific ride builder of this era, patented a system of holding a roller coaster to the track that remains in use to this day. This new system, called under friction, made it impossible for roller coasters to leave the tracks, forever changing the nature of roller coasters from mild-mannered scenic railways to true thrillers.

New technology, such as the wide-scale rollout of under friction roller coasters, converged with the booming economy and the newfound popularity of the automobile in the 1920s to drive the amusement park industry into its Golden Age. As most trolley companies had long since divested their amusement park operations, a whole new generation of entrepreneurs flocked to the industry, building amusement parks that catered to the automobile trade. The automobile led to the closing throughout the country of dozens of smaller amusement parks that were unable to provide large parking lots, but the surviving parks boomed; and thrill rides were the primary draw. America was in a mood to play, and there was an insatiable demand for thrills and entertainment at America's amusement parks.

Business continued booming through the 1920s, and amusement parks were constantly looking for new ways to thrill patrons. Roller coasters became larger and more thrilling, and every year a new ride was introduced to the masses. The Tumble Bug, a large ride featuring cars traveling along a circular undulating track, immediately became a favorite upon its invention in 1925. In 1926, Leon Cassidy constructed the first rail-guided dark ride at Tumbling Run Park in Bridgewater, New Jersey, leading to the formation of the Pretzel Amusement Company, a major manufacturer of dark rides. The Tilt-A-Whirl was also introduced to the midway that year. In 1929, inspired by the Winter Olympic bobsled tracks, Norman Bartlett introduced the Flying Turns—a roller coaster whose trains traveled down a trough rather than on tracks—at Lakeside Park in Dayton, Ohio.

Enterprising businessmen were not the only ones getting involved in the industry. In 1928, Westchester County, New York, recognizing the value of having a recreational community gathering place, acquired a collection of ramshackle amusements along the shores of Long Island Sound and replaced them with Playland. Unlike most amusement parks of the era, which had gradually evolved over several decades, Westchester County carefully laid out Playland to provide the optimal mix of rides and attractions. This precise planning was a predecessor to the design of the large corporate theme parks that would open three decades later. The main attractions were arranged around a lushly landscaped mall, and the kiddie attractions were located in a separate smaller amusement park. In addition to the park's main roller coaster, the Aeroplane, a milder ride, the Dragon Coaster, was located just across the midway. Recreation attractions such as an ice rink, swimming pool, beach, and nature preserve complemented the amusements, and a large parking lot accommodated the growing number of automobiles. Towering above it all was the music tower, which broadcast peaceful music

The original 1928 layout of Playland in Rye, New York, was so successful that it has changed little since.

throughout the park. People flocked to the facility, with attendance the first season reaching 2.8 million. The basic design of Playland has changed little to this day, although many of the rides and attractions have been updated to appeal to new generations.

Hard Times

As Playland was setting new design standards for the amusement park industry, the stock market crash of 1929 drove America into the Great Depression. With unemployment peaking at 33 percent, consumers had little money to spend on entertainment, let alone a day at an amusement park. The Depression took a horrible toll on the industry, and hundreds of parks closed across the country. By 1935, only 400 amusement parks remained open. With capital virtually nonexistent, parks did whatever it took to hang on. Popular strategies to attract crowds included food give-aways and live entertainment, or "flesh shows," as they were known. Not all was bleak, as this became the golden age of big bands, which toured amusement parks from coast to coast. The crowds that big bands attracted to many amusement parks were credited with saving dozens of parks during the 1930s.

Fortunately, things did improve, and amusement parks slowly started to get back on track by the late 1930s. Long-deferred maintenance was performed, and new attractions were added. But dark clouds were looming on the horizon once again. In late 1941, America entered World War II, and soon the resources of the nation were focused on the war effort.

The war was a mixed blessing for the amusement park industry. On one hand, with the economy booming in support of the war effort, patrons flocked to amusement parks located near industrial centers and military installations, providing a much-needed cash infusion for the parks. At the same time, gasoline rationing severely hindered operations at parks not easily reached by public transportation. In fact, many parks closed for the duration of the war and in some cases never reopened. Also, with the nation's industrial output fully focused on wartime production, amusement parks could not add new rides, and material shortages made maintenance of existing rides difficult.

When World War II finally ended, America and the amusement park industry enjoyed a period of postwar prosperity. Attendance and revenues grew to record levels, and new parks opened across America. But the world was a rapidly changing place. Veterans sought to capture their portion of the American dream and start families. Many flocked to the suburbs. Entrepreneurs reacted by developing a new concept that soon

San Antonio's Kiddie Park was the original kiddieland when it opened in 1925.

became as much of a fixture in suburbia as the tract home—the kiddieland, a special amusement park featuring rides just for kids. The concept had actually been developed in 1925, when C. C. Macdonald opened the Kiddie Park in San Antonio, which remains in operation. Kiddielands grew from fewer than two dozen in 1950 to more than 150 operating throughout the country by 1960. They were located primarily in large cities such as New York, Chicago, and Los Angeles. Even the primary monument to suburbia, the shopping center, got into the act as several constructed their own kiddielands, with the first opening at Northgate Mall in Seattle in 1950.

A prime beneficiary of the kiddieland boom was the Allan Herschell Company of North Tonawanda, New York. Founded in 1916 as a manufacturer of carousels, the company started selling kiddie rides following World War II. By 1950, they offered six different types of kiddie rides, and spent much of the decade introducing new models that they aggressively marketed to kiddieland operators. They even put together packages of rides to offer entrepreneurs a turnkey kiddieland operation and published a how-to-guide titled "Kiddielands: A Business with a Future."

Unfortunately, the reality was not as bright as Herschell had hoped. Kiddielands, with their narrow target market and prime real estate, quickly fell out of favor and were largely gone by the early 1970s. Though some grew into full-fledged amusement parks, fewer than a dozen kiddielands from this era remain in operation today, including Pixie Playland, Concord, California; Funland, Idaho Falls, Idaho; Hoffman's Playland, Latham, New York; and Memphis Kiddie Park, outside Cleveland.

As America was flocking to the suburbs, the core of the industry, the large urban amusement park, was being left behind in the face of aging infrastructure, television, urban decay, and desegregation. Coming off the capital constraints of the Depression and World War II, many parks were struggling to update and stay competitive. It seemed that these parks were becoming increasingly irrelevant as the public turned elsewhere for entertainment. What was needed was a new concept to reignite the industry, and that new concept was Disneyland.

The Theme Park Era

By the 1950s, Walt Disney was an internationally renowned filmmaker. He often spent Sunday afternoons with his kids at a local amusement park, lamenting the fact that there was nothing that the family could enjoy together. Disney initially considered building a small entertainment facility at his movie studio, featuring a train, boat and stagecoach rides, a Wild West Town, and a circus. But as his dream grew, so did the size of the project.

When Disneyland first opened in 1955 on a former orange grove in Anaheim, California, many people were skeptical that an amusement park without any of the traditional attractions would succeed. There were no roller coasters, no swimming pool or beach, and no midway games. Instead of a midway, Disneyland offered five distinct themed areas—Main Street, Adventureland, Frontierland, Fantasyland, and Tomorrowland— providing guests with the fantasy of travel to different lands and times. Disneyland was an immediate success, attracting nearly 4 million people in its first year of operation. The theme park era was born.

Robert Ott, former chairman of Dorney Park in Allentown, Pennsylvania, credits Disney with changing many things—"the way parks are organized, cleanliness, the use of lights and colors." Says Ott: "He catered to the customers, made them happy. His magic flowed into amusement parks. We all benefited from it." Carl Hughes, chairman emeritus of Kennywood in West Mifflin, Pennsylvania, one of America's best remaining traditional parks, concurs: "The standards changed. You couldn't get away with dirty midways and surly employees." It was a whole new era in the amusement park industry.

Although Disneyland is often given credit for being the first theme park, the concept had actually been evolving for more than a decade before Disneyland, as several smaller attractions opened that embraced a single theme. Many of these attractions, which helped inspire Disney, are still in operation today. These include Knott's Berry Farm in Buena Park, California, which started building its Ghost Town in 1940; Holiday World (originally Santa Claus Land), which opened in 1946 in Santa Claus, Indiana; Santa's Workshop, North Pole, New York, which started in 1949; Santa's Village, which opened in Jefferson, New Hampshire, in 1953; and Storyland in Glen, New Hampshire, and Great Escape (formerly Storytown USA) in Lake George, New York, which both opened to visitors in 1954.

As important as the opening of Disneyland was, Ott remembers another event that was also important in changing the face of the industry in the 1950s. In 1958, the industry trade association, then known as the National Association of Amusement Parks, Pools, and Beaches, took a tour of Europe. Since the European industry was largely wiped out during World War II, it had been rebuilding with a level of sophistication not yet found in American parks—intricate flower beds, elaborate landscaping, and flashy new rides adorned with thousands of electric lights. "That trip changed the industry," Ott recalled. "We brought back new and more sophisticated ideas." Although these new ideas created an even more complex industry in America, implementing them was quite expensive. For parks struggling to come back from the Depression and World War II, it was too much.

The excitement created by Disneyland and the ideas from Europe opened a new era for amusement parks, but the industry suffered some growing pains. A variety of parks attempted to cash in on Disney's concept, but many lacked the appeal of Disney or simply did not have the financial resources. In 1958, Magic Mountain opened west of Denver when it was only partially completed, and it closed almost immediately. It later reopened and now exists as a shopping village and amusement park. Pacific Ocean Park, widely credited with making the pay-one-price admission an industry standard, opened in Ocean Park, California, in 1958 with the backing of CBS, but it closed in 1968 due to high maintenance bills. Pleasure Island debuted near Boston in 1959, but it could never get its main attraction, a giant robotic replica of Moby Dick that was supposed to rear out of a body of water, to work properly. It closed in 1969, never achieving its hoped-for popularity.

But the most spectacular failure was Freedomland in the Bronx. Built in the shape of the United States, the park opened in 1960, incomplete and over budget. From the beginning, it was plagued by accidents, poorly planned attractions, insufficient capacity, and a robbery. Furthermore, the park was constructed atop a former landfill on improperly graded land. The buildings shifted as they settled and required expensive repairs. The park struggled on until 1964, when it collapsed under a mountain of debt.

It wasn't until 1961, when Six Flags Over Texas opened between Dallas and Fort Worth, that another major theme park was finally successful. Backed by the land development firm Great Southwest Corporation, the park was the first in what today is the largest theme park chain in the world. Six Flags adapted traditional amusement park rides to a theme park, introducing the log flume to the industry in 1963 and building the first Runaway Mine Train roller coaster in 1966. Following on the success of Six Flags, which proved that the theme park was a viable concept apart from Disney, theme park development during this time took off. Between 1964 and early 1965, fifteen theme parks opened, and *Amusement Business* reported that twenty additional projects were in the works. Although these tended to be smaller, short-lived roadside attractions, the success of Six Flags caught the attention of major corporations, such as Clairol, Penn Central, ABC, Marriott, Taft Broadcasting, and Mattel, which were soon planning their own parks. Even Bob Hope considered opening a theme park in Los Angeles in the 1960s. Among the major parks opening during this time were the first Sea World theme park, which debuted in San Diego in 1964; Six Flags Over Georgia in Atlanta in 1967; Astroworld in Houston in 1968; Magic Mountain near Los Angeles, Six Flags Over Mid-America outside St. Louis, and the

Freedomland in New York City was one of the many failed attempts to duplicate the success of Disneyland.

immense Walt Disney World in Florida, all in 1971; and Opryland in Nashville in 1972. What these parks had in common was a location close to interstate highways on the outskirts of town, high standards of design and operation, and disdain for traditional amusement park attractions such as wooden roller coasters and midway games.

That disdain, however, changed in 1972 when Taft Broadcasting opened Kings Island near Cincinnati. Kings Island was different from most theme parks. Its roots were found in a very successful traditional amusement park—Coney Island in Cincinnati—which had been regarded as one of the most successful and best-run amusement parks in the country. Walt Disney even visited Coney Island to observe its operations while planning for Disneyland. Its success was a double-edged sword, however, because it became increasingly difficult to accommodate growing crowds in its cramped location on the Ohio River. In addition, flooding was a constant nuisance. As a result, in 1969 it was decided to relocate the park to a larger site in the suburbs, where it would become a major theme park. Given Coney Island's success, its owners had no reservations about including traditional amusement park attractions, even persuading renowned roller coaster designer John Allen to come out of retirement and build two wooden roller coasters—the twin-track Racer and the smaller Scooby Doo (now the Fairly Odd Coaster). The new park was called Kings Island.

The Racer at Kings Island, outside Cincinnati, introduced the wooden roller coaster to the theme park.

People flocked to Kings Island and lined up for hours to ride the Racer. Kings Island proved that people were still longing for traditional thrills, and the industry responded by opening more theme parks. In 1973, Carowinds opened near Charlotte, followed by Great Adventure in New Jersey and Kings Dominion near Richmond in 1974; Busch Gardens in Williamsburg, Virginia in 1975; and Minneapolis's Valleyfair and the two Great America parks in California and Illinois in 1976. While these parks continued to embrace many of the design standards of their earlier cousins, their resistance to more traditional amusement park rides was not as strong as had been the case with their predecessors.

Trying to Compete

While theme parks increasingly dominated the industry in the 1960s and 1970s, the old traditional parks were facing hard times. Several factors made it difficult for many parks to compete in this new climate. Aging rides and buildings were in need of expensive upgrades, and the growing sophistication of attractions at the theme parks made new attractions increasingly expensive to both purchase and maintain. The congested urban location of many of the older parks made expansion difficult, and urban decay often caused the loss of family business. Finally, increasing land values prompted many park operators to sell their facilities to developers. As a result, the industry saw the sad closings of many large urban traditional parks—parks that used to be the cornerstones of the industry.

Not all was bleak, however. Many traditional amusement parks learned from theme parks and revitalized their operations. One of the most dramatic examples was Cedar Point, located halfway between Cleveland and Toledo in Sandusky, Ohio. Once known as the "Queen of American Watering Places," by the late 1950s the park was a shell of what it had been earlier in the century. In 1957, investors purchased the attraction with the intention of redeveloping the park. A local outcry persuaded them to retain the amusement park and rebuild it, using flashy new theme park–style rides and adding themed areas. By the 1970s, Cedar Point was widely recognized as one of the most successful amusement parks. Building on this success, the owners purchased a theme park, Minnesota's Valleyfair, in 1978. Today CedarFair, as the company is now known, is a billion dollar operation, owning or managing twelve amusement and theme parks and six water parks. Cedar Point was not the only example of a traditional park successfully adapting to a theme park environment. Hersheypark in Pennsylvania revived its business by adding a series of themed areas. Other parks, such as Kennywood in West Mifflin, Pennsylvania; Geauga Lake in Aurora, Ohio; Riverside (now Six Flags New England) in Agawam, Massachusetts; and Lagoon in Farmington, Utah, maintained their traditional atmosphere but incorporated ideas pioneered by theme parks, including uniformed employees, live entertainment, costumed characters, and theme park–style rides such as log flumes, observation towers, and monorails.

Palisades Park in New Jersey was one of the greatest of the urban traditional parks to close in the 1960s and 1970s.

Competition and New Concepts

Theme park development slowed dramatically by the late 1970s, simply because most of the markets large enough to support such a facility now had a park. As a result, most theme park operators concentrated on expanding and improving existing facilities. Most attention was focused on topping one another with record-breaking roller coasters. Sparked by the interest generated by Kings Island's Racer, the seventies saw a roller coaster arms race. New record-breaking heights were achieved, and in 1975, Knott's Berry Farm and Arrow Development Corporation built a steel corkscrew looping roller coaster. Soon looping roller coasters were must-have attractions for successful theme parks. The intense competition sparked innovations in ride technology, which reached a level of complexity never before experienced. Most rides were now computer controlled and made by new high-tech manufacturing processes.

This was all extremely expensive, and rapidly increasing manufacturing costs coupled with a downturn in the industrial economy—which provided the picnic business that so many traditional parks relied upon—brought about another wave of park closures in the late 1970s. By the end of the decade, nearly 100 amusement parks had closed forever.

Geauga Lake in Aurora, Ohio, broke new ground in 1983 when it became the first amusement park to combine traditional rides with water park attractions.

As the industry entered the 1980s, opportunities for new theme parks were limited, and the demand for large thrill rides was waning due to an aging population and increasing costs. The popularity of water attractions skyrocketed during the decade, however, as they could be enjoyed by the entire family and provided a fun way to cool off on a hot summer day. New concepts included the river rapids (introduced in 1980), the splashwater (1984), and the "dry" water slide (1986). It was an era of tremendous growth for water parks, which eschewed traditional rides for water slides. The first water park, Wet 'n Wild, opened in Orlando in 1977, but the concept truly took off in the 1980s. By 1983, water parks were so popular that Geauga Lake in Aurora, Ohio, became the first amusement park to add a full-scale water park to its lineup of traditional amusement park attractions. Now it is rare that a theme or amusement park does not include a water park as part of its offerings.

The ride simulator was another attraction that many amusement parks thought would be the wave of the future during the 1980s. Small versions such as the Astroliner had been available since 1978, but the opening of Star Tours at Disneyland took the experience to an entirely new level. Industry observers predicted that simulators would supplant traditional thrill rides, because they could easily be reprogrammed into a new ride experience every few years. Most major theme parks added a simulator, but the lines at the roller coasters did not grow any shorter.

Many American theme park operators also turned their attention overseas. Disney became the first major American operator to expand overseas, opening Tokyo Disneyland in Japan in 1983. It soon became the world's most popular amusement park and set off a wave of theme park construction in Asia, turning it into the second-largest amusement park market in the world. In the 1990s, a similar phenomenon occurred in Europe, with Disney opening Euro Disneyland in 1992. Soon other American operators such as Busch Entertainment Corporation, Six Flags, and Universal Studios tested the waters in competition with several European-based theme park developers with limited success.

The Industry Today

By the late 1980s, amusement park operators realized something very surprising: As the "baby boom" generation got older, they were not retiring from enjoying thrill rides like previous generations had done. The roller coaster innovations in the late 1970s failed to satiate their appetite for thrills, and in 1988 the arms race began anew with the construction of the 170-foot-tall Shock Wave at Six Flags Great America in Gurnee, Illinois. It held the record for only a year, however. The following season, Cedar Point in Sandusky, Ohio, constructed Magnum XL 200, the first

The Shock Wave at Six Flags Great America in Gurnee, Illinois, reignited the roller coaster arms race when it opened in 1988.

roller coaster to surpass 200 feet in height. The arms race continued for the next decade and a half, peaking in the year 2000, when over 100 roller coasters opened around the world. In fact, that year the world's record for the largest and fastest roller coaster changed hands three times—from Goliath at Six Flags Magic Mountain (255 feet tall and 85 miles per hour) in February, to Millennium Force at Cedar Point (310 feet tall and 92 miles per hour) in May, to Steel Dragon at Nagashima Spa Land in Japan (318 feet tall and 95 miles per hour) in August. That record stood until 2003, when Cedar Point opened Top Thrill Dragster, which stands 420 feet tall and has a top speed of 120 miles per hour. Again it was topped in 2005 with the opening of Kingda Ka at Six Flags Great Adventure in New Jersey, at 456 feet tall and 128 miles per hour. As for Shock Wave, the ride that reignited the arms race, it was dismantled in 2002 and sold for scrap as a result of declining popularity.

The year 1988 was also significant in that the development of new theme parks in the United States resumed, some being built in cities that had been considered too small for such an attraction in the 1970s. These included Sea World Texas in San Antonio (1988); Wild Adventures, Valdosta, Georgia (1991); Six Flags Fiesta Texas, also in San Antonio (1992); Visionland (now Alabama Adventure), near Birmingham, Alabama (1998); Legoland, near San Diego (1999); and Hard Rock Park, Myrtle Beach, South Carolina (2008).

Enthusiasts' Groups

There are dozens of organizations for people interested in amusement parks or just specific rides. The largest of these include:

American Coaster Enthusiasts (ACE)

1100-H Brandywine Boulevard
Zanesville, Ohio 43701-7303

www.aceonline.org

Publications include *Roller Coaster!*, a quarterly magazine, and *ACE News*, a bimonthly newsletter. Normally hosts four national events and several regional events annually in North America.

Dark Ride and Fun House Enthusiasts

P.O. Box 484
Vienna, Ohio 44473-0484

www.dafe.org

Publishes *Barrel of Fun*, a quarterly newsletter, and hosts at least one event a year.

The Dark Ride and Fun House Historical Society

22 Cozzens Avenue
Highland Falls, New York 10928

www.laffinthedark.com

Features online newsletter.

European Coaster Club

Six Green Lane
Hillingdon, Middlesex
UB8 3EB England

www.coasterclub.org

Publishes *First Drop*, a bimonthly magazine, and hosts six to eight events a year, mostly in Europe.

National Amusement Park Historical Association (NAPHA)

P.O. Box 871
Lombard, Illinois 60148-0871

www.napha.org

The only club following all aspects of the amusement and theme park industry. Publishes *NAPHA News*, a bimonthly magazine, and *NAPHA NewsFLASH!!!*, a monthly newsletter. Hosts two events annually, primarily in North America.

(continued on page 22)

Enthusiasts' Groups

(continued from page 21)

National Carousel Association

Barbara May, executive secretary
P.O. Box 19039
Baltimore, Maryland 21284-9039

www.nca-usa.org

Membership benefits include the quarterly magazine,
Merry-Go-Roundup, a biennial census report of
existing carousels and a biennial membership
listing. Hosts an annual convention and
a technical conference.

Roller Coaster Club of Great Britain (RCCGB)

P.O. Box 235
Uxbridge, Middlesex UB10 0TF
England

www.rccgb.co.uk

Publishes *Airtime*, a bimonthly newsletter,
and a yearbook. Hosts six to eight events
a year, primarily in Europe.

There is also a wealth of clubs around the world targeting specific regions or interests. These include: CoasterBuzz Club, Coaster Enthusiasts of Canada, Coaster Zombies, Florida Coaster Club, Great Ohio Coaster Club (GOCC), Mid Atlantic Coaster Club (MACC), Western New York Coaster Club (WNYCC), Wild Ones Coaster Club (Pacific Northwest).

In the 1990s, the amusement park industry enjoyed a level of prosperity not seen since the 1920s. Theme parks were opening around the world and attracting record numbers of people. Although some parks did close, the traditional parks that survived the hard times have learned to compete and have become beloved local institutions.

The distinction between theme and traditional parks has become blurred, with theme parks adding thrill rides that have little connection to their original themes and traditional parks adding themed areas. And the two have always shared a desire to entertain their customers and respond to an ever-changing society.

Consumers seemed to have less free time available for entertainment in the 1990s, so the industry responded with a new concept: the family entertainment center. Unlike larger parks, which required one or two days to fully enjoy, family entertainment centers emphasized activities that could be enjoyed in a short amount of time. Most cities now feature one or more of these facilities, which can range from a large game arcade to a miniature amusement park complete with go-carts and kiddie rides.

Although the industry is increasingly dominated by major corporations and large, high-tech thrill rides, there is a renewed sense of appreciation for the industry's heritage. Two amusement parks—Pittsburgh's Kennywood and Playland in New York—are now listed as national historic landmarks, as are numerous rides throughout the country, such as the Giant Dipper roller coaster at a revived Belmont Park in San Diego and Leap-the-Dips at Lakemont Park in Altoona, Pennsylvania, both saved due to grassroots preservation efforts. A few parks, most notably Arnold's Park in Iowa and Conneaut Lake Park in Pennsylvania, have found new life as nonprofit community assets. The few remaining family-owned parks have found ways to peacefully coexist with the large, corporate-owned competitors.

In the twenty-first century, the industry has consolidated into a few major players that dominate the business, while rising real estate values have led to a new wave of amusement park closings even engulfing theme parks such as Astroworld in Houston and Libertyland in Memphis. Despite this, the industry is enjoying unprecedented popularity. In all corners of the world, people flock to their local parks in record numbers, and thanks to advances in technology, they are thrilled in ways never before imagined—400-foot-tall roller coasters with speeds exceeding 100 miles per hour; linear induction motors launching rides at unheard-of acceleration rates; 300-foot-tall free falls; and dark rides in which riders become part of the action. More than 300 million people flock to American amusement parks annually, which is more than twice the number in 1970, despite the fact that the number of parks has remained consistent at around 600. The industry seems to have entered a new golden age.

A History of the Amusement Park
in Virginia, Maryland, and Delaware

THE REGION THAT COMPRISES THE STATES OF VIRGINIA, MARYLAND, AND Delaware, along with the District of Columbia, represents a cross section of America. From the miles of seashore that define its eastern edge to the mountains of the west; from the megalopolis that starts in Wilmington and runs through Baltimore, Washington, and Richmond to the Hampton Roads area, to the small cities such as Roanoke and Cumberland tucked into the Blue Ridge Mountains; from action-packed boardwalks in Rehoboth Beach, Ocean City, and Virginia Beach, to secluded tourist getaways—this is an area that can offer something to almost everyone.

With its northern border consisting of the famed Mason-Dixon Line, the region has traditionally been the transitional region between the northern and southern United States. Like many of its northern brethren, Baltimore was a key player in the industrial revolution, but Richmond was the capital of the Old South. Another characteristic that this area inherited from the south was its legendarily steamy summers. These summers were the leading influence in the birth of the region's amusement park industry.

A Place to Escape

In the 1870s, fledgling transportation companies saw an opportunity to transport people out of sweltering city centers to cool getaways in the country. Although development in Virginia was slow as a result of its smaller population and ongoing recovery from the Civil War, Washington, D.C., and Baltimore provided fertile ground for entrepreneurs.

The banks of the Potomac River were a particularly appealing refuge. One of the region's first amusement parks was Cabin John Park, which opened in 1876, as part of the Cabin John Hotel, located just about nine miles upriver from Washington in Maryland. An upscale resort with well-manicured grounds, the facility featured one of the first carousels carved by Gustav Dentzel, among the most renowned carousel carvers in history. Cabin John Park remained in operation until 1910 when it was eclipsed by newer resorts.

About 25 miles down the Potomac from Cabin John, Marshall Hall, a tobacco plantation dating back to 1690, started hosting picnics in 1876. According to legend, George Washington originally tried to acquire the property for his own plantation before settling for Mount Vernon across the river. Initially, access to Marshall Hall was limited to those who could make the carriage ride out to the property, but in 1889, the Mount Vernon Steamboat Company, which ran steamboat excursions down the Potomac, acquired the property and began offering direct access from Washington. Marshall Hall turned into a full-fledged amusement park and operated for the next ninety years.

But the residents of Washington were not the only ones to be offered the opportunity to escape the summer heat. In 1871, the newly formed Western Maryland Railway selected a site in the Blue Ridge Mountains of northern Maryland, seventy-one miles from Baltimore, for the future location of an amusement park to help finance the railroad's western expansion. By August 1877, Pen Mar Park, so named due to its proximity to the Pennsylvania-Maryland border, opened for business on top of a mountain at an elevation of 1,400 feet. Not only did it offer a spectacular view of 2,000 square miles of countryside, but its key draw was a temperature that was at least ten degrees cooler than the streets of Baltimore.

Growth quickly came to the park. Observation towers were erected on nearby mountain tops in 1878 and 1879 and accessed from the park via carriage rides. Rides followed including a carousel in 1907 and a roller coaster in 1909. By then, the self-proclaimed "Coney Island of the Heights" attracted daily crowds of up to 20,000 to enjoy the cool, secluded mountain getaway.

Of course, early amusement park growth was not limited to inland areas. The shores of the Chesapeake Bay in Maryland provided ample opportunity for people to escape the heat. Tolchester Beach was one of the first. Located along the Eastern Shore, the park was opened by the Tolchester Steamboat Company in 1877. Originally the location was supposed to be used as a transfer point for passengers and cargo to a proposed railroad. But when the railroad went bankrupt prior to completion, the docking facilities were converted into an amusement resort.

The Switchback roller coaster was a popular attraction at Tolchester Beach, one of the region's first waterfront resorts.

Initially, Tolchester Beach covered just 10 acres, but it quickly grew to encompass 155 acres with six steamers providing service to as many as 20,000 visitors a weekend. The state's first horse track opened there shortly after the turn of the twentieth century, followed by the park's two great wooden roller coasters, the Switchback and Whirlpool Dips, in 1909 and 1913. Tolchester Beach achieved notoriety in 1889 when it put an embalmed whale on display and gave people the opportunity to have tea inside its mouth.

Across the bay near Annapolis, Bay Ridge opened in 1879 with steamboat service from Baltimore and Annapolis. Traffic grew to the point where the Bay Ridge and Annapolis Railroad established service in 1886. Its attractions included one of the region's first roller coasters, the Switchback Railway, erected around 1888 by LaMarcus Thompson. Bay Ridge remained a popular resort until closing in 1903.

The last of the great Chesapeake Bay resorts to open was Chesapeake Beach. It was originally proposed in 1891 as the "Monte Carlo of the East." After initial plans fell through, a new investor group, the Chesapeake Beach Railway Company, took over the project in 1896 and in 1900 succeeded in completing a 28-mile rail line from Washington, D.C., to the community. When it opened, the resort consisted of a mile-long boardwalk filled with rides and concessions, along with a long pier for strolling and fishing. Steamboats carrying excursionists from Baltimore docked at the end of the pier.

By the Sea

The Atlantic shore was also a popular respite from the region's summer heat, and the area's seaside resorts got their start during this time. Ocean City, Maryland, was first when according to legend, Isaac Coffin built a beachfront cottage to receive paying guests in 1869. Customers arrived by stagecoach and ferry to fish and enjoy the cooling effects of the ocean. In 1875, the town was incorporated and the first hotel opened. It was followed by the completion of a rail trestle across Sinepuxent Bay, linking the town to the railroad in 1876. Daniel Trimper opened his amusement park in 1893, followed by Ocean City Pier in 1907, five years after the first boardwalk was constructed by several oceanfront hotel owners to relieve their guests from the tiring walk through sand. Both Trimper's amusement park and the pier remain in operation.

Just 25 miles to the north, Rehoboth Beach, Delaware, was founded in 1873 as a Methodist Episcopal Camp, featuring the region's first boardwalk, an 8-foot-wide, 1,000-foot-long path of oak planks. The arrival of the railroad in 1878 changed the personality of the community as the influx of summer vacationers resulted in the religious camp being discontinued in 1881. The following year, Charles Horn constructed the town's first amusement facility, Horn's Pavilion, on a 150-foot-long pier. The popular attraction was destroyed by a hurricane in 1914.

Seaside Park was built by the Norfolk and Southern Railroad in 1912 as the first amusement park in Virginia Beach.

Railroads also played a key role in the development of Virginia Beach, Virginia. In 1883, the completion of a 19-mile railroad line from Norfolk to the Atlantic coast established the area as a resort destination. Hotels and cottages began to line the shore and in 1888, an 8-foot wide, 4-block-long boardwalk connecting two major hotels was completed.

But although Virginia Beach was established as a resort about the same time as its brethren to the north, it took longer for amusements to be established there. That was solved in 1912 when the Norfolk and Southern Railroad opened Seaside Park along the oceanfront. It was an elaborate facility covering two blocks and featuring three connected pavilions containing a ballroom, restaurants, a carousel, and eventually a roller coaster.

The End of the Line

Ironically, the region that gave the nation the first practical electric-powered street rail line did not feel the influence of the trolley park as profoundly as states such as Pennsylvania and Ohio. But nonetheless, the development of amusement parks at the end of trolley lines in Virginia, Maryland, and Delaware was a key reason that the number of amusement parks in the region more than doubled during the first decade of the twentieth century from fifteen to thirty-six.

Baltimore, then one of the largest cities in the country, saw the most significant trolley park development. Gwynn Oak Park was the city's earliest and longest lived. Its genesis was a decision by a group of housing developers to offer 64 acres of land free to the Baltimore & Powhatan Railroad for an amusement park to induce them to build a trolley line to the parcel.

Gwynn Oak, which opened in 1895, had a more sedate atmosphere than many of its peers that offered concerts, sports activities, and theater. In fact, the park's first roller coaster did not even appear until 1909. Customers had to maintain a "high moral tone." Alcohol was forbidden as was tobacco consumption by women, and dancers could not get too close.

River View Park, which was opened in 1898 by the United Railways Company, had actually been a popular beer garden dating back to 1868. It continued that tradition as a trolley park, making alcohol readily available, creating a much more raucous atmosphere than other parks. It grew into the "Coney Island of the South" featuring three major roller coasters along with a full selection of other rides.

Baltimore's other great trolley park, Bay Shore Park, had a completely different tone than its competition. Built in 1906 by the United Railways and Electric Company, the 32-acre facility on the shores of the Chesapeake was billed as the "Atlantic City of Maryland." It featured large ornate buildings, including a concert hall, hotel, and a high-class restau-

Baltimore's Bay Shore Park was one of the largest trolley parks to operate in the region.

rant along with a white sand beach and a pier extending into the bay. As the *Baltimore Sun* reported on opening day, "the buildings are commodious and handsome. They are substantially constructed, nothing cheap. At night the thousands of electric lights, studded here and there with an arc light, produce a superb effect."

Trolley park development was much more limited in Washington, where Glen Echo Park quickly established itself as the city's leading trolley park. The facility dated back to 1889 when the Baltzley brothers purchased 516 acres outside town in Maryland to create a new community. In 1891, they opened a chautauqua, a summer cultural camp, on a portion of the property. Several stone buildings were erected including an amphitheater, restaurant, and hall of philosophy. Although the chautauqua only lasted one season, other groups used it until 1899 when it was leased to a new company that converted what was then known as Glen Echo Park into an amusement facility.

The new management ran into a certain level of controversy in 1906 when the manager of the park wanted to expand onto neighboring property owned by Red Cross founder Clara Barton. She refused to sell and the park tried to drive her out by erecting a roller coaster and a Ferris wheel next to her house. This management style brought the park to the brink of financial ruin, and in 1909 the Washington Railway and Electric Company purchased the park and added a number of new rides, leading it to a long and successful life.

For much of its existence, Brandywine Springs was the leading amusement park in Delaware. The park actually predated the trolley park era opening in 1886 when Richard Crook took over operation of the Brandywine Springs Hotel and added picnic grounds in a cool wooded grove. He soon followed up with a merry-go-round, a dance pavilion, sports attractions, and in 1890 the Toboggan Slide roller coaster. A trolley line linked Brandywine Springs to Wilmington in 1898 and with the opening of a new Scenic Railway roller coaster in 1903, it became the leading facility in the area.

The park's fortune took a turn in 1915, when its parent company, the People's Railway Company, was acquired by the Wilmington and Philadelphia Traction Company, which owned Shellpot Park. For many years Shellpot Park operated in the shadow of Brandywine Springs. But with the purchase, the company focused its efforts on Shellpot Park and Brandywine Springs closed in 1923.

Farther south in Richmond, trolley park development finally reached that city during the first decade of the twentieth century. Idlewood Park was the city's best-known trolley park, originally opening in 1906. Its features included a horse show pavilion, a carousel, and a roller coaster. Although 20,000 people showed up at the park its first July Fourth, Idlewood's fame was fleeting. The park went bankrupt in September 1908; and, in 1910, the city tried to close it. New ownership in 1911 attempted

The Toboggan Slide was an early roller coaster at Wilmington's Brandywine Springs Park. The ride opened in 1890.

Idlewood Amusement Park was the leading trolley park in Richmond during the early twentieth century.

to revive the operation by building a new roller coaster, but the investment failed and the park quietly shut in 1914.

Outside of the big cities, trolley park development was quite limited as most communities were too small to have any sort of meaningful trolley system. The longest-lived trolley park in this area was Braddock Heights Park in Braddock Heights, Maryland, which was opened in 1896 by the Hagerstown and Frederick Railway. Located on a mountain top, it featured an observation tower, along with a hotel, a carousel, a summer theater, a roller skating rink, and a bowling alley. When trolley service ended in 1947, the park went into a decline and quietly closed in 1964.

The trolley park also made its way to Roanoke, Virginia, where the Roanoke Street Railway Company opened Mountain Park in 1902. In addition to the standard attractions such as a roller coaster and a dance pavilion, Mountain Park built an incline railway in 1909 offering trips to the top of the mountain that towered over the amusement park.

Although transportation companies were the dominant driver of amusement park development in the region in the late nineteenth and early twentieth centuries, entrepreneurs did build a few parks.

Along the shores of Hampton, Virginia, the Sembler family purchased a 15-acre site on the Chesapeake and built a bathhouse, promoting the beach as a place to cool off. In 1898, they sold it off to Frank Darling, who launched a major expansion with a new bathhouse, a hotel, a the-

Bird's-Eye View looking South across Chesapeake Bay, Buckroe Beach, Va.

9A-H1517

Buckroe Beach Amusement Park in Hampton, Virginia, was started by entrepreneurs in 1896.

ater, and rides, leading to a long, successful run as Buckroe Beach Amusement Park.

Baltimore's Electric Park originally started in 1896 as a picnic park with a trotting track. As its name implied, electricity was the park's main attraction with thousands of electric lights adorning the rides and buildings. As the industry matured, Electric Park evolved into an exposition park in the mold of Coney Island's Luna Park, featuring elaborate live shows such as a simulated Johnstown Flood, a fighting flames show, a Wild West show, and a baby incubator. But like so many parks of its genre, the high overhead of its attractions took its toll. The rides were closed in 1913 as the park focused on horse racing, and the entire facility shut in 1915.

The region's other exposition park was Luna Park in Arlington, Virginia, which opened in 1906. It was built by Frederick Ingersoll, who had already established himself as a well-known builder of roller coasters, and was part of the first chain of amusement parks, foreshadowing Six Flags by more than half a century. Like its sister parks in Pittsburgh and Scranton, Pennsylvania; Cleveland; and Mexico City, it featured exotic architecture, rides, a circus arena, and live shows. Unfortunately, Ingersoll's complex parks, packed into confined urban locations, required almost constant upgrades. By 1908, Ingersoll was bankrupt; and, in 1915, Arlington's Luna Park was demolished.

A New Wave

After the initial flurry of development, openings of amusement parks in Virginia, Maryland, and Delaware slowed appreciably in the 1910s with the number of parks in the region remaining steady at around thirty. As the teens morphed into the twenties, many of the region's older parks succumbed to the newfound popularity of the automobile, which made trips to larger, more distant resorts possible.

Roanoke's Mountain Park went under in 1923 after several years of declining business. Island Park in Hagerstown, originally built by the Baltimore and Ohio Railroad in 1879, was destroyed by a flood in 1924 and never rebuilt. Richmond's Forest Hill Park closed in 1925 after two decades of operation. The largest park to close during the era was Baltimore's River View, which had trouble adapting to the automobile era. After 1929, United Railways, looking to get out of the business, sold the land to Western Electric for room to expand its neighboring plant.

While older parks were closing, a new generation of entrepreneurs was jumping into the industry to take advantage of the automobile culture. One of Baltimore's most well-known amusement parks was opened in 1919 when John Carlin decided that an amusement park was the best way to generate revenue on a vacant property he owned. Originally known as Liberty Heights Park and later just Carlin's, the 70-acre facility was reflective of the era with its intense focus on rides, chief among

29:- BIRD'S-EYE VIEW AMUSEMENT SECTION CARLIN'S PARK, BALTIMORE, MD.

44451

Carlin's Amusement Park was one of the numerous amusement parks opened by entrepreneurs following World War I.

them being the Mountain Speedway. Regarded as one of the top roller coasters of its time, the 4,500-foot-long ride was known for its 800-foot-long tunnel and a trip through a ravine. A 1923 visit by Rudolph Valentino caused a mob scene and the actor had to be sneaked into the park. In 1930, a life-size mechanical elephant caught fire and burned, making Carlin's home of Baltimore's only known elephant fire.

Out near Roanoke, the void created by the fading Mountain Park was soon filled by Lakeside Park, which opened outside town in Salem in 1920. Developed by a local department store executive, the park was like many others developed in the 1920s, using a 300-by-125-foot, 2-million-gallon swimming pool as its main attraction. A major expansion in 1924 resulted in Lakeside becoming a full-blown amusement park with the construction of the Wildcat roller coaster.

Along the Atlantic shore, the New Ocean Casino, which opened in Virginia Beach in 1924 as a competitor to Seaside Park, had a saltwater swimming pool, a dance hall, and rides, but never achieved the level of success as Seaside Park and closed in the years following World War II.

The Quiet Years

Like the rest of the country, the amusement industry in Virginia, Maryland, and Delaware entered a quiet period in the 1930s as the Depression made it difficult for parks to expand. In fact, the number of parks in the region fell from thirty-two in 1925 to approximately nineteen in 1939.

The largest park to close during the 1930s was Shellpot Park in Wilmington, Delaware. Following the closing of longtime rival Brandywine Springs in 1923, Shellpot launched a major expansion that included the construction of the Wildcat, a major wooden roller coaster, in 1925. In January 1934, however, the park was severely damaged by a fire. The struggling economy could not justify repairing the damage to the park, which was only partly covered by insurance; and it never reopened.

The World War II years provided additional challenges for the region's amusement parks in the form of material shortages and travel restrictions. Some parks such as Chesapeake Beach shuttered for the duration. But Pen Mar Park probably suffered the most. The mountain getaway had been struggling since the automobile became popular in the 1920s. In the spring of 1943, wartime restrictions shut down the railroad and gas rationing meant people could not drive there, resulting in the park's ultimate demise. In 1977, Pen Mar Park reopened as a county park so that new generations could enjoy its spectacular scenery.

While many parks struggled, others boomed. There were probably few parks in the country that benefited as much from the war as Ocean View Park in Norfolk, Virginia. The park originally opened in 1899 to

AMUSEMENT SECTION, PEN.MAR, PA.

Pen Mar Park, one of the oldest amusement parks in the region, was forced out of business by rationing during World War II.

generate traffic on a rail line that connected the oceanfront to downtown Norfolk. By 1905 its first roller coaster opened and in 1928, Otto Wells purchased the facility and launched a major expansion program. Included was a kiddieland complete with one of the first true kiddie coasters, a fun house, and other major rides. But the centerpiece of the expansion was the Skyrocket, a 90-foot-tall wooden roller coaster—known for its large drops—that soon achieved legendary status in the region. By that time Ocean View Park was known as the Atlantic City of the Southland, but it would not last.

A 1933 storm destroyed Ocean View Park's oceanfront boardwalks and, combined with the Depression, led to the closing of the park in the late 1930s. In 1942 Dudley Cooper purchased the 25-acre site as a real estate investment, but the Navy urged him to reopen the park as a recreation center. Due to coastal blackout restrictions, a 12-foot-tall canvas screen was erected for half a mile along the shore to shield the lights of the park. Since Norfolk was the primary point of debarkation for amphibious troops heading overseas, business boomed and Ocean View Park thrived throughout the war.

Out with the Old, In with the New

The years following World War II saw many of the parks that had anchored the industry from its earliest days start to fall by the wayside for a variety of reasons. The first to go was Baltimore's Bay Shore Park. Although it successfully bounced back from a major fire in 1941, its neighbor, Bethlehem Steel Corporation, eyed the property to expand its massive plant. In 1947 the company reached an agreement to acquire the facility as part of a larger 900-acre purchase. The expansion never came to fruition and the land sat abandoned until 1987 when the state took it over for a recreational area, restoring the old trolley shed and fountain.

Although Bay Shore was gone, former park owner George Mahoney could not bear to be out of the business and opened a new Bay Shore Park in 1948. Originally envisioned as the first phase of a 250-acre resort that would cover three islands in the Chesapeake, it was connected to the mainland by a 1,220-foot-long bridge and featured the largest beach in Maryland.

Unfortunately, the new Bay Shore Park lacked the grand scale of its predecessor, was difficult to get to, and never achieved the same level of success. Although the rides closed in the late 1950s, the remaining attractions did not close until 1964 when that property was also taken over by Bethlehem Steel.

Near Washington, D.C., Great Falls Park in Fairfax, Virginia, one of the region's early trolley parks, finally closed in 1952 after forty-six years of operation. Its long decline started during the Depression. Fairfax County took over the faded facility and converted it into a county park.

The 1950s also saw the demise of another of Baltimore's once great amusement parks. Plagued with fires throughout much of its existence, Carlins's started losing business after World War II; with revenues declining, maintenance was deferred. Fires in November 1955 and January 1956 resulted in a limited schedule in 1956 with no rides in operation and by the next season the park was converted into a drive-in theater.

Another park that faded away during this time was Tolchester Beach, one of the region's oldest facilities. The park had been suffering since automobiles made it easier for people to travel to more distant resorts. The Depression led to the bankruptcy of its steamboat company, and World War II made it difficult to make improvements. Its Switchback roller coaster was removed in 1949, the deteriorated Whirlpool Dips closed in 1959, and in 1961 the hotel was condemned and torn down while the carousel was given to creditors in lieu of payment. New owners came and made grand plans to build a modern resort; but by 1962, the fading park was bankrupt, and it closed forever.

But all was not bleak during this time. In the years following the war, returning veterans sought to capture their share of the American dream by moving to the suburbs and starting families. This created a need for family-type entertainment near their suburban homes and places to go to on weekend road trips, which led to the development of two new genres of amusement parks; the kiddieland and the themed roadside attraction. This helped to drive an increase in the number of parks in the region from twenty-one in 1955 to thirty-four in 1966.

Kiddielands, scaled-down amusement parks located along busy suburban streets, provided a quick, easy, and inexpensive entertainment option to growing postwar families. Although they were not as common in Virginia, Maryland, and Delaware as in other major cities, approximately ten opened throughout the region in the 1950s and 1960s. They tended, however, to be short-lived attractions succumbing to the pressures of rising land values after only a few seasons. Kiddieland in Baltimore was one of the first, opening in 1950. Kiddie Town in Wilmington, Delaware, was a little more successful, operating from the early 1950s until the late 1960s. One of the last to go was Kiddieland in Takoma Park, Maryland, which opened in 1960 and held on until the early 1970s.

In the Washington, D.C., area, the kiddielands that opened, including Fun Fair in Falls Church, Peppermint Ranch Kiddie Park in Arlington, and Arlandia Kiddieland in Alexandria, tended to only last a few seasons.

Like kiddielands, themed roadside attractions established themselves in the region during the 1950s and 1960s, but not to the extent in the more densely populated states to the north. The oldest and most beloved was Enchanted Forest, which opened in Ellicott City, Maryland, just outside Baltimore on August 15, 1955, just one month after Disneyland changed the industry.

The park was developed by Howard Harrison Sr., father of five and grandfather of eleven. He had long dreamed of a place were people could relive beloved fairy tales. In 1953, after a careful evaluation, Harrison acquired a 20-acre farm and brought his dream to life on a rolling wooded section of the property. Patrons entered through a 40-foot-tall, 35-foot-wide castle and experienced twenty displays, as well as live characters and animals. Unlike most parks of the time, there were no mechanical rides.

Enchanted Forest was a huge hit and the *Today* show broadcasted from the park, attracting national attention. Increasing traffic prompted a 12-acre expansion in 1962 that featured the introduction of several mechanical rides. The park became a beloved attraction for generations of Maryland residents, but by the 1980s, aging facilities and increasing land values caught up with the park. It closed in 1988 and a shopping center was developed on much of the property. Five acres consisting of most of the original storybook attractions were retained and reopened in 1994. It failed to recapture the magic and closed after a single season. In recent years, many of the storybook attractions have been relocated to the nearby Clark's Elioak Farm.

Enchanted Forest's successful opening was followed by parks such as the still-operating Frontier Town in Ocean City, Maryland, which opened

Enchanted Forest opened in 1955 outside Baltimore and became one of the region's most beloved theme parks before closing in 1994.

in 1959; Story Book Land, which operated from 1959 until 1981 in Woodbridge, Virginia; Frontier City, which entertained visitors in Virginia Beach from 1960 until 1961, and Old Virginia City of Fairfax, Virginia, which opened in 1960 and operated throughout much of the 1960s.

Although kiddielands and themed attractions dominated development in the 1950s and 1960s, that did not mean that traditional amusement park development ground to a halt. With the spread of interstate highways, seaside resorts such as Virginia Beach and Ocean City were introduced to larger crowds of tourists. In Virginia Beach, a group of entrepreneurs opened Playland in 1966, but the park failed after only a single season. Ocean City saw two major parks open in 1965. One, Jolly Roger Park, has continued to thrive and remains in operation. The other, Playland, was a large facility that featured nearly two dozen rides. Originally, Playland resembled a shopping mall consisting of a series of tenant operators. But the unique business model had a hard time getting established at its location well away from the main tourist area. Although management was able to stabilize the situation, the park closed in 1980 and was purchased by the city for a public works facility.

A Separate World

As previously mentioned, Virginia, Maryland, and Delaware form the transitional region between the northern and southern United States. One of the unfortunate side effects of this role was that for much of its existence, the amusement industry was highly segregated. Although African-Americans were not permitted in the same amusement parks that white people patronized, they were not entirely excluded. From the 1890s until the 1970s, approximately ten parks in the region were opened to cater to African-American patrons.

The earliest such park was Notley Hall Amusement Park in Prince George's County, Maryland, outside Washington, which opened in 1894. Like many early parks, it was connected to the city by steamboat and offered a bowling alley, horseback rides, swings, and a carousel. It operated until 1924.

Like the industry as a whole, the 1920s was an active decade for amusement parks catering to African-Americans. The year 1921 saw two such amusement parks open in the region. In Baltimore, Wonderland opened on a 14-acre site and featured a large wooden roller coaster among its attractions. Unfortunately, it was plagued by fires during its existence and was auctioned in 1929.

In Washington, D.C., Suburban Gardens was opened by the Universal Development and Loan Company, a black-owned real estate development corporation. The only major amusement park to operate in the District, it covered 7 acres and featured a dance pavilion, a swimming pool, and a roller coaster. Suburban Gardens operated until 1940.

Brown's Grove was another popular destination that enjoyed its heyday in the 1920s. Located in Rock Creek, Maryland, it was served by a steamboat piloted by Capt. George Brown and advertised as "the only park in the State of Maryland run exclusively for Colored People and by Colored People." Attractions included the Racer Dip roller coaster.

African-American amusement parks were not just limited to the big cities in the region. Seaview Beach opened in Lynnhaven, Virginia, in 1947 on the shores of the Chesapeake to provide an oceanfront amusement park to those who were not allowed in facilities elsewhere. Ironically, the amusement park was owned by Dudley Cooper who operated nearby Ocean View Amusement Park in Norfolk and Seaside Park in Virginia Beach, both of which were segregated. To his credit, Cooper hired African-Americans to manage and staff the facility. Seaview Beach was best-known for its dance hall, which featured topflight entertainment such as Cab Calloway.

The last to open of the region's amusement parks catering to African-Americans was Carr's Beach in Annapolis, Maryland. Opening in the 1950s, its amusement area was rather modest in scale. What it was known for was its dance hall whose leading acts such as James Brown, Ray Charles, Ella Fitzgerald, and Chuck Berry attracted crowds from miles around. Carr's Beach lasted until the early 1970s.

By the time Carr's Beach was in its prime, however, the Civil Rights movement was in full swing. Throughout the country, people of all races marched side by side to demand full and equal access to all facilities for all people. This included the amusement park industry. Separate facilities would no longer do and the reaction varied widely.

On one extreme was Mago Vista Beach. Located along the banks of the Magothy River near Annapolis, the park opened in 1938. Not only was the park racially segregated, but a sign at the entrance read "Gentiles Only." Rather than integrating, management shuttered the park in 1964 and sold the property.

Mago Vista Beach's story barely resonated compared with the challenges that the two largest parks in the region faced in the 1960s. Glen Echo Park, outside Washington, D.C., had continued to thrive, becoming one of the best-known parks in the country. The Coaster Dips, a large wooden roller coaster built in 1921 that traveled through a ravine was regarded as one of the best around. Its carousel, carved in 1921 by William Dentzel, was one of the most beautiful in the country, and the 1931 Crystal Pool and 1933 Spanish Ballroom packed in revelers.

But in 1960, Howard University students began picketing the segregated park and were arrested after attempting to ride the carousel. At the time the state and county government were of little assistance, asserting they had little control over a privately owned facility. But supporters of integration, black and white, held firm and launched petition drives and daily protests that resulted in dozens of arrests.

The pressure continued, and in 1961 Glen Echo Park opened for the season to all races. Integration went well. The feared clashes did not materialize and the owners responded by continuing to add new rides. Early in the 1966 season, however, an overcrowded spring day resulted in a number of disturbances in the park. Glen Echo started to close attractions in an

attempt to clear the facility, but there was insufficient bus service to transport crowds out of the neighborhood and vandalism spread outside the park. The resulting publicity scared off family trade and the park became a hangout for teenage gangs. After the park closed in 1968, the owners made plans to erect apartments on

Glen Echo Amusement Park, outside Washington, D.C., closed in 1968 due to unrest following desegregation.

Unique and Historic Attractions

Carousel, Trimper's Rides, and Amusements
This ride is one of the finest examples of the carousel art. Hand carved in 1902 by the Herschell Spillman Company, this large ride has remained in its original location since then. Unlike most carousels, Trimper's model features a menagerie of animals including cats, dogs, frogs, zebras, giraffes, mules, ostriches, pigs, roosters, a camel, a deer, a lion, a stork, a tiger, and an elaborate dragon. A full-time curator ensures that the ride is kept in pristine condition.

Curse of DarKastle, Busch Gardens Europe
This is one of the most unique dark rides in the country. Curse of DarKastle takes riders into the legend of King Ludwig by using cutting-edge technology. Boarding Golden Sleighs, riders journey through his castle where they are menaced by skeletal knights, a giant wolf, and King Ludwig's severed head.

Eiffel Tower, Paramount's Kings Dominion
This 330-foot-tall structure is a one-third scale replica of the original Eiffel Tower in Paris and is the defining icon of this theme park. The observation deck on the top provides a spectacular view of the park and surrounding countryside.

Haunted House, Trimper's Rides and Amusements
An excellent example of a classic amusement park dark ride from the 1960s, Trimper's two-story Haunted House was originally built by Bill Tracy, one of the leading attraction designers of the era.

Haunted Mansion, Funland
One of the best traditional dark rides in the country, the Haunted Mansion is tucked into a hidden second floor at this compact seaside amusement park. A unique suspended transportation system and abundance of surprises make this a ride with few peers.

Kiddie Rides, Trimper's Rides and Amusements
Trimper's Rides and Amusements is home to one of the largest and best-preserved collections of kiddie rides from the 1920s. Built by the William F. Mangels Company of Coney Island, New York, which invented the kiddie ride, the park's Fairy Whip, dry boats, Ferris wheel, fire engines, and merry-go-round are all lovingly maintained antiques that remain as popular as the day they opened.

Merry-Go-Round, Six Flags America
Although this is a newer ride, being manufactured in 1981, it is a one of a kind merry-go-round featuring panda bears, and African animals such as camels, rhinos, and ostriches, rather than the horses traditionally found on merry-go-rounds.

(continued on page 42)

Unique and Historic Attractions
(continued from page 41)

Pirate's Cove, Trimper's Rides and Amusements
This large walk-through attraction was built by master designer Bill Tracy and is one of only two of his walk-through attractions still in operation.

Steam Train, Frontier Town
Built in 1961 by Crown Metal Products of Wyano, Pennsylvania, Frontier Town's miniature train is one of a fading number of miniature trains in amusement parks that are steam powered.

Wild One, Six Flags America
The Wild One is a classic roller coaster dating to 1917, when it opened at Paragon Park, Hull, Massachusetts. When that park closed in 1984, it was relocated to Maryland and carefully restored to thrill a new generation of riders. One of the few wooden roller coasters successfully relocated from another location, it remains a crowd favorite.

the site; but the locals did not want to lose the prime property overlooking the Potomac River to private uses. As result, the 17-acre site was acquired by the National Park Service, which reopened it as an arts center in 1971. Today the carousel continues to spin; and many of the buildings, including the Spanish Ballroom and bumper car pavilion, have been restored for a new generation.

Unfortunately, the situation ended differently for Gwynn Oak Park in Baltimore. The park had been taken over from the trolley company in 1936 by the Price family who built it into a Baltimore institution. By the time the Big Dipper roller coaster opened in 1957, the park was already under pressure to integrate. As local schools and companies stopped having picnics at the park, the Price family resisted, claiming they had the right to operate their facility as they saw fit. But on July 4, 1963, in an incident commemorated in the John Waters film *Hairspray*, a demonstration at the front gate resulted in 300 arrests. On August 28, the decision was made to integrate Gwynn Oak.

Although the integration in 1963 was too late in the season to measure its impact, the 1964 season saw mixed results. The return of corporations and schools led to a large increase in picnic business, but the walk-in trade fell. Few incidents were reported. But in 1966, a parking lot disturbance resulting from a lack of bus transportation at the end of the day signaled the beginning of the end. The Price family stopped making improvements, blaming integration for chasing away the family trade and making it uneconomical to invest in the increasingly deteriorating facility.

On June 22, 1972, Hurricane Agnes roared through Baltimore covering Gwynn Oak Park in up to five feet of water. Damage totaled $1.5 million and thirteen rides were destroyed. Although an attempt was made to reopen, the park could not get an operating permit and only the ballroom reopened. By 1974, the shuttered facility was foreclosed upon and soon demolished and converted to a city park. Today, only the carousel remains. Manufactured in 1948 by the Allan Herschell Company, the sixty-horse ride was one of the largest merry-go-rounds made since the end of World War II. It was purchased by the Smithsonian Institution and now operates on the National Mall in Washington, D.C.

Variations on a Theme

Integration was not the only change rocking the amusement park industry. Ever since Disneyland changed the industry in 1955, theme parks were spreading throughout the country. With its dense population base, the corridor extending from Baltimore to Richmond attracted numerous theme park developers. Some succeeded, such as Taft Broadcasting, which opened Kings Dominion north of Richmond in 1974; and Anheuser-Busch, which developed Busch Gardens Europe in Williamsburg, Virginia, in 1975. The ABC Wildlife Preserve, which the television network opened outside Washington in 1974, initially failed and struggled to find its place until its successful conversion to Six Flags America in 1999. But for the most part, the many theme park proposals barely made it out of the planning stage.

Although parks such as Heritage Gardens—which was proposed in 1968 for a 149-acre site in Washington—and the Marriott Corporation's planned Great America park came and went quietly in the wake of funding shortages and planning problems, the region was home to what was likely the most contentious battle over a theme park ever fought in the United States.

In November 1993, the Walt Disney Company stunned the industry by announcing plans to construct a theme park in Haymarket, Virginia. The $625 million, 3,000-acre development was to include office, retail, and residential space; 1,300 hotel rooms; and a convention center along with a 400-acre theme park celebrating "the nation's richness of diversity, spirit and innovation." It sought to combine traditional rides with historical reenactments in nine themed areas including ones devoted to the presidents, Native Americans, the Civil War, the nation's immigrant heritage, the industrial revolution, and agriculture.

But from almost the time the announcement was made, opposition groups formed. They were concerned that the park would only be 4 miles from Manassas National Battlefield Park and claimed that the development would destroy the rural atmosphere of the area. Others were opposed to America's challenging history being used in theme park attractions.

By March 1994, the state approved $163 million to improve roads around the site and opponents raised $1 million for their fight. Included in the opposition group were area landowners such as Robert Duvall and Jacqueline Kennedy Onassis and historians such as Shelby Foote and David McCullough, who claimed Disney "would create synthetic history by destroying real history."

As the project continued to work its way through the approval process, opponents succeeded in getting a hearing in the Senate, while a resolution was introduced in the House. On September 17 opponents marched down Pennsylvania Avenue in the nation's capital. Days later Disney announced plans to cancel the project, concluding that fighting the opposition would be too costly, create too many delays, and tarnish the company's reputation. Initially they said that they would seek a new site and offers came in from other states. But the plan soon faded away.

Even though Disney's America failed to become a reality, the region grew into one of the largest theme park destinations in America, with three of the industry's largest operators—Busch Entertainment, Cedar-Fair, and Six Flags—being represented.

The End of an Era

As the region was growing into a theme park mecca, however, all was not well with the remaining traditional parks that managed to survive the tumultuous 1960s and 1970s. By the end of the 1980s, the increasing competition from theme parks, combined with the need for costly upgrades led to the closing of all but Trimper's Rides and Amusements in Ocean City, Maryland, and Funland in Rehoboth Beach, Delaware.

The end of the 1972 season saw the loss of two once-popular Chesapeake Bay resorts. Cottage Grove Beach, which opened in 1904, hosted its last visitors, as did Chesapeake Beach—once one of the region's largest resorts. After a series of storms and fires in the 1920s, this park was moved from its original bay side location farther inland in 1930. In 1946, new owners took over the facility and launched a renovation of the amusement park. The 1952 opening of the Chesapeake Bay Bridge made the seashore more accessible, leading to a drop in patronage, but the outlawing of slot machines, a crucial revenue source, in 1968 was the final blow. Fortunately, its magnificent hand-carved carousel survived the closure and now operates at Watkins Regional Park in Largo, Maryland.

Marshall Hall Amusement Park faded away in 1978. Since the 1930 construction of a wooden roller coaster on the property, the amusement park on the banks of the Potomac River had thrived. In 1966, new own-

Chesapeake Beach in Maryland was one of the many older amusement parks to close in the 1970s and 1980s.

ers launched a modernization of the old park. Unfortunately, it was the scene of a riot in 1968 following the assassination of Martin Luther King Jr. But the owners were undaunted and in 1969 proposed converting Marshall Hall into a "Spirit of America" theme park. The proposal was met with immediate opposition from area residents who were working to assemble land for a park that would preserve the view from Mount Vernon across the river from Marshall Hall. Zoning for the theme park was rejected in 1971.

This launched a three-year battle between the park and the government with the park cutting down trees along the shore of the river and threatening to erect a 250-foot-tall observation tower. Finally in 1974, the National Park Service received authorization to purchase land and incorporate it into Piscataway Park. The park was given five more years to operate.

Unfortunately, during the lengthy battle, Marshall Hall's owners failed to invest in the facility and it became increasingly run down. Paint was peeling and the motor on the carousel fell apart; in the final blow, on July 7, 1977, a windstorm knocked down the lift hill on the roller coaster. The splintered debris that was the roller coaster remained at the park during what would be the park's last year in 1978.

Although Marshall Hall's demise was almost merciful, the closing of Norfolk's Ocean View Park, that same year was much sadder. Under the guidance of the Cooper family, the park continued to maintain its high standards, making it one of the most popular amusement parks on the east coast. In 1970, Ocean View had its best season with over a million visitors. But soon, the park started losing money in the face of rising costs and theme park competition. Not even a featured role in the 1977 movie *Roller Coaster* could turn things around and in 1978, the Coopers sold the 14-acre park to the city of Norfolk.

The shuttered amusement park caught the attention of Playboy Productions, which thought its demolition would be the perfect plot of a movie. The result was the *Death of Ocean View Park,* a 1979 made-for-television production in which a hurricane damages a natural gas line in the park leading to a series of explosions that destroy the facility. The demolition of the renowned Skyrocket roller coaster was to take a leading role, but the ride was not about to go quietly. A first attempt with seventy-six sticks of dynamite and hundreds of gallons of gasoline did little damage. A second try with more explosives only succeeded in blowing out the windows of a shopping center across the street. The producers finally had to cut the ride's main supports and pull it over with a bulldozer in conjunction with an explosion.

Although Ocean View Park went out with a bang, its longtime competitor, Buckroe Beach Park in nearby Hampton, closed just a few years later with a whimper. The park had steadily grown since the 1920s when it added a new carousel from the Philadelphia Toboggan Company in 1920 and the Dips roller coaster in 1921. In 1953, the Steffen family purchased the park

The legendary Sky Rocket roller coaster was destroyed for the movie Death of Ocean View Park *following the park's closure in 1978.*

Gone but Not Forgotten

Although the Virginia, Maryland, and Delaware area is still blessed with a wealth of amusement parks, all too many are now memories. Throughout its history, over 200 different amusement parks have operated in the region. Here is a list of some of the better known ones.

Aqua-Land Park, Newburg, Maryland, early 1960s to late 1960s.
Arlandria Kiddieland, Alexandria, Virginia, early 1960s to late 1960s.
Arlington Beach, Washington, D.C., early 1920s to late 1930s.
Augustine Beach Amusement Park, Port Penn, Delaware, late 1940s to early 1960s.
Bay Ridge Resort, Annapolis, Maryland, 1879 to 1903.
Bay Shore Amusement Park, Baltimore, Maryland, 1906 to 1947.
Bethesda Park, Bethesda, Maryland, 1891 to 1894.
Braddock Heights Park, Braddock Heights, Maryland, 1896 to 1964.
Brandywine Springs Park, Wilmington, Delaware, 1886 to 1923.
Buckroe Beach, Buckroe Beach, Virginia, 1896 to 1985.
Byrnes Island Park, Hagerstown, Maryland, 1879 to 1924.
Cabin John Park, Glen Echo, Maryland, 1876 to 1910.
Carlin's Amusement Park/Liberty Heights Park, Baltimore, 1919 to 1955.
Carr's Beach, Annapolis, Maryland, 1950s to 1970s.
Casino Park, Virginia Beach, Virginia, 1924 to late 1940s.
Chesapeake Beach, Chesapeake Beach, Maryland, 1900 to 1929.
Chesapeake Beach–Seaside Park, Chesapeake Beach, Maryland, 1930 to 1972.
Colonial Beach Park/Reno Amusement Park, Colonial Beach, Virginia, late 1920s to 1982.
Cottage Grove Beach and Amusement Park, Pasadena, Maryland, 1904 to 1972.
Deemer Beach, New Castle, Delaware, late 1920s to early 1950s.
Electric Park, Baltimore, 1896 to 1912.
Enchanted Forest, Ellicott City, Maryland, 1955 to 1989.
Family Funjungle, Ellicott City, Maryland, 1992 to 1994.
Flood's Park, Maryland, 1908 to 1916.
Frederick Road Amusement Park, Baltimore, 1920 to 1925.
Frontier City, Virginia Beach, Virginia, 1960 to 1964.
Glen Echo Park, Glen Echo, Maryland, 1891 to 1968.
Great Falls Park, Fairfax, Virginia, 1906 to 1952.
Gwynn Oak Park, Baltimore, 1895 to 1972.
Idlewood Park, Richmond, 1906 to 1914.
Jeepers!, Baltimore, 1998 to 2001.
Jeepers!, Glen Burnie, Maryland, 1998 to 2001.
Jeepers!, Norfolk, Virginia, 1999 to 2006.
Kiddie Town, New Castle, Delaware, early 1950s to late 1960s.
Kiddieland, Takoma Park, Maryland, 1960 to early 1970s.
Lakeside Park, Salem, Virginia, 1920 to 1986.
Loop Amusement Park, Virginia Beach, Virginia, 1974 to 1975.
Luna Park, Danville, Virginia, late 1930s to mid-1960s.
Luna Park, Arlington, Virginia, 1906 to 1915.
Luna Park/Paragon Park, Baltimore, 1910 to late 1910s.
Mago Vista Beach, Annapolis, Maryland, 1938 to 1964.
Marshall Hall Amusement Park, Marshall Hall, Maryland, 1876 to 1978.

(continued on page 48)

Gone but Not Forgotten
(continued from page 47)

Mountain Park, Roanoke, Virginia, 1902 to 1923.

New Bay Shore Park, Baltimore, 1948 to 1964.

Notley Hall Amusement Park/Washington Park, Prince George's County, Maryland, 1894 to 1924.

Ocean View Park, Norfolk, Virginia, 1899 to 1978.

Old Virginia City, Fairfax, Virginia, 1961 to late 1960s.

Pen Mar Park, Pen Mar, Maryland, 1877 to 1942.

Peppermint Ranch Kiddie Park, Arlington, Virginia, late 1950s to mid-1960s.

Playland, Rehoboth Beach, Delaware, late 1920s to 1961.

Playland, Ocean City, Maryland, 1965 to 1980.

Playland, Virginia Beach, Virginia, 1966 only.

Ponyland, Bailey's Road, Virginia, early 1960s to late 1960s.

Regal FunScape, Wilmington, Delaware, 1996 to 2000.

Regal FunScape, Chesapeake, Virginia, 1995 to 2000.

River View on the Potomac, Prince George's County, Maryland, 1895 to 1918.

River View Amusement Park, Baltimore, 1898 to 1928.

Seaside Amusement Park, Virginia Beach, Virginia, 1912 to 1986.

Seaview Beach, Lynnhaven, Virginia, 1947 to 1964.

Shellpot Park, Wilmington, Delaware, late 1800s to 1933.

Story Book Land, Woodbridge, Virginia, 1959 to 1981.

Suburban Gardens, Washington, D.C., 1921 to 1945.

Tolchester Beach, Tolchester Beach, Maryland, 1877 to 1962.

Wonderland Park, Baltimore, 1921 to 1929.

and launched a major improvement program that included a kiddieland and the Cascades water ride. Through the 1950s and 1960s, the park enjoyed its golden age; but pressures began mounting. It struggled through integration, theme park competition, and the decision by the city to redevelop the area for residential rather than resort uses. The park began losing money in 1968 and attendance fell to less than a hundred thousand annually. The family quietly closed the park in 1985. Today, the land is a public beach, and its antique carousel operates in downtown Hampton.

The next year, the amusement era in the Tidewater region seemed to come to an end as its last remaining park, Seaside Park, shuttered after seventy-four years of operation. The park had been declining in both size and stature since a fire hit the facility in 1956. Over the next three decades, it gradually gave way to development in the area, with its final parcel closing in 1986.

At the opposite end of the state, Lakeside Park in Salem also entertained its last visitors in 1986. Since its opening in 1920, it had grown into the leading amusement park in western Virginia. A major modernization program in the late 1960s culminated with the 1968 construction of the Shooting Star. One of the few wooden roller coasters being built at the time, it was a large ride standing 90 feet tall with 4,120 feet of track.

The new roller coaster helped park attendance reach 450,000 in the early 1970s. But soon attendance went into a decline. The park went through a series of owners in the 1980s and attendance fell to just 150,000. In 1985, a flood caused $2 million in damage to the park. The owners launched a fund-raising effort by selling passes to local residents and were able to repair much of the damage for the 1986 season. Unfortunately, an employee was killed in a freak accident and Lakeside Park could not recover. The traditional amusement park era in Virginia, Maryland, and Delaware had largely come to an end.

A New Age

By the 1990s, there were only about a dozen amusement parks in the region, but the densely populated, tourist-rich region was fertile ground for new concepts being introduced to the industry. One such concept was family entertainment centers, which sought to appeal to time-pressed families with experiences that could be enjoyed in a few hours.

Like theme parks in the 1970s, a number of different companies tried their hand at the family entertainment center business. One was Regal Cinemas, one of the largest movie theater operators in the country. They saw an indoor version of a family entertainment center as a way to capture a larger portion of revenue from moviegoers. As a result, they opened Regal FunScape centers as part of theaters in Chesapeake, Virginia (1995), and Wilmington, Delaware (1996), featuring attractions such as indoor go-cart tracks, bumper cars, miniature golf, and simulators. But as they soon discovered; operating a family entertainment center was not the same as operating a movie theater, and Regal closed both facilities in 2000.

Salem, Virginia's Lakeside Park was the last of the region's big amusement parks to close in the 1980s.

Another variation was the indoor kiddie park, focusing on rides and activities for smaller kids. The region probably saw more of them than any other developed in the 1990s. Approximately ten opened, about the same as the number of kiddielands that operated in the region during the 1950s and 1960s. The largest operator was the Jeepers! chain, which developed seven centers in the Baltimore and Washington areas between 1996 and 1998. But again, the operators soon discovered that it was difficult to attract enough customers outside evenings and weekends to keep the building operating, and most were closed by 2001. Today, just one remains in operation in the region.

Although indoor centers had limited success, more traditional outdoor family entertainment centers quickly established themselves in the region with two, Go-Karts Plus in Williamsburg, Virginia, and Adventure Park USA in New Market, Maryland, receiving recognition from the International Association of Amusement Parks and Attractions as among the finest family entertainment centers in the world.

Family entertainment centers have dominated growth in the region in recent years, but a few traditional amusement parks also opened. Responding to the need for family activities in the resort, the Tidewater area saw the return of the seaside amusement park with the opening of Boardwalk Amusements in 1995 and Virginia Beach Amusement Park in 2000. Meanwhile, Blue Diamond Amusement Park opened in 2004 outside Wilmington, Delaware, reintroducing the roller coaster to Delaware for the first time since 1933.

Over its 130-year history, the amusement industry in Virginia, Maryland, and Delaware has seen many changes and faced many challenges. One thing has remained constant, however—that sense of escape. People once sought the mountains and the shore to escape stifling summer heat, people now seek to escape the pressures of everyday life by being transported for a day to another place at a world-class theme park, being swept up in the excitement of the seashore, or just taking a couple of hours to ride a go-cart or play miniature golf with a friends and family at an award-winning family entertainment center. The more things change, the more they stay the same.

Trimper's Rides and Amusements

OPENED 1893

IT IS NO SURPRISE THAT THE OCEAN CITY OF DANIEL TRIMPER'S DAY IS vastly different from the town of today. The once sleepy village now sprawls several miles along the Atlantic coast. The cottages and hotels have been replaced by towering condominiums. A sunny summer weekend attracts 300,000 visitors. The boardwalk he and other local businessmen laid out in 1902 now stretches nearly 3 miles along the ocean.

But Daniel Trimper would not feel totally lost in this bustling resort. The carousel that he risked his entire fortune on a century ago still thrills young and old alike. The antique kiddie rides he purchased in his later years look as good as the day he bought them, and the Atlantic Ocean still serves as a welcome respite on a hot summer day.

Daniel Trimper's legacy, Trimper's Rides and Amusements, is a microcosm of Ocean City—an exhilarating mix of old and new.

Embracing an Opportunity

Daniel B. Trimper and his wife Margaret were living the American dream. German immigrants, they embraced the opportunities their new home gave them by working at local amusement parks, operating a concession stand on a steamer, and eventually owning their own bar in Baltimore—the Silver Dollar. In 1890, the couple journeyed to the young summer resort of Ocean City, which had slowly been gaining popularity since the railroad came to the town in 1879. They were enam-

Trimper's Rides and Amusements
South 1st Street and the Boardwalk
Ocean City, MD 21842
410-289-8617
trimpers@dmv.com
www.beach-net.com/trimpers/

ored with the fledgling community and in 1892 made the fateful decision to sell their business in Baltimore and move to Ocean City.

They purchased two blocks in the town, which at the time consisted more of dreams than actual structures. Included in the deal were two of the town's three hotels—the Sea Bright and the Eastern Shore. That winter, they loaded their ten children on a steamer for the trip across the Chesapeake Bay. As they neared the harbor, the boat encountered ice and the family had to disembark and haul their belongings across the ice to the shore for the final leg of their journey.

Settling into their uncompleted house behind Sea Bright Hotel, they set out to build a new life in the rustic settlement. Although there were three hotels, the town had fewer than fifty permanent residents, no street lights, and just two mail deliveries a week.

But Trimper knew that the beach would prove to be an unbeatable attraction and teamed up with his brother to make the most of the opportunity. A theater was soon erected near the hotels to show movies and vaudeville acts, and the first ride was added, a primitive carousel powered by two men.

The fledgling operation soon became a hub of the young town, but in 1900 Trimper's was faced with a major challenge when a storm washed the front of the Sea Bright hotel into the ocean. Inspired by previous travels to Europe, Trimper took the opportunity to rebuild the hotel as

Daniel Trimper's Windsor Resort became a fixture on the Ocean City boardwalk by the turn of the twentieth century.

 **VISITING**

LOCATION

Trimper's Rides and Amusements is located at the southern tip of Ocean City, along the boardwalk between South Division and South 1st Streets. From U.S. Route 50, cross the H. Kelly Memorial Bridge over Sinepuxent Bay. Turn right on Philadelphia Avenue to South First Street. Look for the Tidal Wave roller coaster.

Pay parking is available at the municipal lot across the Boardwalk from the amusement park.

OPERATING SCHEDULE

The indoor rides at Trimper's are open weekends throughout much of the year at 1 P.M. Outdoor rides open for the season at 1 P.M. on weekends anywhere from late March to the first of May depending on the weather.

The park begins full-time operations in mid-June with all rides and attractions open at 1 P.M. on weekdays and noon on weekends. Closing is typically around midnight, but can vary depending on the size of the crowd. Full-time operations typically end in late August, with weekend hours through the fall.

ADMISSION

Admission to the park is free. Visitors have a choice of paying by the ride or purchasing a one-price wristband. Ride tickets cost approximately 40 cents each with rides taking between three and eight tickets.

The pay-one-price wristband costs under $25 and permits visitors to enjoy all rides and attractions between the hours of noon and 6 P.M. on weekends and 1 P.M. to 6 P.M. on weekdays. Evening hours (after 6 P.M. to closing) are not included.

FOOD

Trimper's Rides and Amusements features two food stands, both called the Red Apple, with locations on the boardwalk and in the main outdoor ride area. Both feature hot dogs, popcorn, cotton candy, and other snack items.

In addition, the Trimper's Inlet Village shopping area is home to two restaurants—Harrison's Harbor Watch and the Red Eyed Frog Café.

Don't miss the variety of food concessions located along the boardwalk. Highlights include Dolle's Candyland, which has been selling saltwater taffy and other treats since 1910; Dumser's Dairyland, which has been serving ice cream on the boardwalk since 1939; Phillips Restaurant, known for its seafood; the Dough Roller for pizza and pancakes; and Thrashers, serving its legendary french fries since 1929.

FOR CHILDREN

Trimper's Rides and Amusements features a wide array of kiddie and family rides. The carousel building is home to most of the kiddie rides, along with the carousel. Outside, the park has numerous rides the entire family can enjoy including the Wacky Worm roller coaster, the Flying Tigers, the Balloons, and several fun houses.

(continued on page 54)

VISITING (continued from page 53)

SPECIAL FEATURES

Trimper's carousel is one of the finest and best-preserved examples of the carousel art. Dating back to 1902, the ride is one of the few antique carousels to feature a wide variety of animals.

The park contains the largest collection of antique kiddie rides found anywhere. Largely manufactured by the William F. Mangels Company of Coney Island, New York, the rides represent a living museum of kiddie rides. Dating back to the late 1910s and early 1920s, the five rides (a Ferris wheel, fire engines, land boats, a merry-go-round, and a whip) look as good as the day they opened. Don't miss the kiddie whip with its beautiful hand-painted murals on each car.

The Haunted House dark ride is one of the best dark rides around and was originally built by Bill Tracy, the leading dark ride designer of his era.

Few amusement parks have the variety of walk-through attractions as Trimper's. These include Pirate's Cove, one of only three walk-through attractions remaining designed by Bill Tracy, one of the greatest attraction designers of his era; the Aladdin's Lamp fun house, a European import; a classic Mirror Maze; and two smaller attractions.

TIME REQUIRED

To fully experience Trimper's Rides and Amusements, four hours should be sufficient, although the major attractions can be enjoyed in about two hours. Visitors should, however, plan to spend the day in Ocean City and enjoy the beach and all of the boardwalk attractions.

TOURING TIPS

To avoid crowds, visit the park during the afternoon, particularly on weekdays. If you plan to ride extensively, be sure to go in the afternoon when pay-one-price wristbands are available.

Remember, the carousel, bumper cars, and eleven kiddie rides are all located indoors. So don't let inclement weather spoil your day.

The Haunted House is located along the boardwalk, away from the other rides. Don't miss it.

the Congress Hall. It was decorated with turrets giving the property a resemblance to Windsor Castle, leading to the naming of Trimper's holdings as Windsor Resort.

By now Windsor Resort was the anchor of the growing town. The human-propelled merry-go-round was replaced by a larger version. It was powered by a steam engine that was also pressed into service to create electricity for the operation. It was the first electricity in town and an attraction in its own right, with people coming just to see the lights.

In 1902, Daniel Trimper teamed up with several other businessmen in town to lay down a series of planks along the sand in front of their operations to make it easier for customers to walk along the beach and not track sand into the businesses. At first it was a temporary assemblage that was taken up during high tides. But in 1910 a permanent boardwalk was erected, the beginning of Ocean City's now legendary 3-mile long promenade.

Adding an Icon

With Trimper's operation now attracting more and more people, the merry-go-round was soon inadequate. As a result, he decided to risk everything by acquiring a carousel unlike any seen before in that part of the country. Trimper contracted with the Herschell Spillman Company of North Tonawanda, New York to manufacture the machine. With a diameter of 51 feet, it was one of the largest carousels built up until that time, featuring a menagerie of animals arranged in three rows. In addition to twenty-three hand-carved horses, the carousel features cats, dogs, frogs, zebras, giraffes, mules, ostriches, pigs, roosters, a camel, a deer, a lion, a stork, a tiger, and an elaborate dragon, along with three chariots and one large rocking chair. To ensure the ride would open for tourist season, Herschell Spillman sent the partially completed ride to Ocean City with a crew of carvers so that the animals could be installed as they were finished.

A large waterfront building was erected to house the ride and protect it from the ocean elements. To this day it forms the core of the amuse-

Trimper's carousel has been the heart and soul of the amusement park since 1902.

ment park. Since then, the ride has not been moved from this original location, and has become the heart and soul of the operation.

When it first opened, the new carousel was powered by a steam engine, but as the entire town was electrified, the steam engine was retired. According to legend, it was too large to remove from the building and was buried underneath the present location of the bumper car ride.

In the years following World War I, the William F. Mangels Company in Coney Island, New York, changed the industry by inventing the kiddie ride. Parks around the country soon jumped at the chance to add attractions that their youngest visitors could enjoy. Trimper's was one of the first, purchasing several of Mangels's offerings including a kiddie whip, a Ferris wheel, a merry-go-round, boats, and fire engines. All were installed in the building surrounding the carousel, providing a place for families to go no matter what the weather. Today, all of these rides remain in operation and are as popular as ever. They are more than rides; they are looked upon as cherished heirlooms and are cared for in such a manner.

The 1920s opened with the development of a new outdoor amusement area south of the carousel building called Trimper's Luna Park. Located along the boardwalk, it was originally anchored by a Ferris wheel and swing ride.

As the 1920s came to an end, Trimper's Windsor Resort underwent a period of transition. The Congress Hall hotel burned in 1927; and in

The Fairy Whip is one of the kiddie rides added following World War I. It continues to be a favorite attraction.

NEW AMUSEMENTS AND BOARD WALK, OCEAN CITY, MD.

Trimper's Luna Park was the name of the outdoor amusement area in the 1920s. The 1933 hurricane largely destroyed this area.

1929, Daniel Trimper died leaving control of the thriving operation he had built to his son Daniel Jr.

But although these were notable developments, a storm in August 1933 impacted not only Trimper's but all of Ocean City. A record storm surge inundated the town, damaging most of the buildings and wrecking a mile-long section of boardwalk. Although Trimper's carousel building survived the pounding, other portions of the complex were not as fortunate. A second major building containing a roller rink was demolished, and the Luna Park section including a Whip ride, which had replaced the swings several years earlier, was washed into the ocean. Making the best of the situation, the Trimpers later salvaged the rink's maple flooring to use on the family home.

Elsewhere in Ocean City, the railroad trestle, which linked the town to the mainland, was destroyed, ending train service to the community. But by now the automobile had taken over as the preferred method of travel to Ocean City, minimizing the impact of the loss. What did have a great impact, however, was the inlet that the storm surge cut through the town, taking part of the Trimper's properties in the process. For several years community leaders had been petitioning the government to create such an inlet to link the ocean with Sinepuxent Bay, facilitating the movement of boat traffic.

Fortunately Mother Nature took care of that for the community. As a result, other improvements were also taken to preserve the inlet and increase the width of the beach, meaning that the Trimpers and other property owners no longer had to worry about closing their buildings when the tide came in too high. With the larger beach, a better environment for boaters, and easy automobile access, Ocean City as a resort was entering its golden age.

Passing the Torch

Despite the growing popularity of Ocean City as a resort, the next three decades were relatively quiet for the Trimper's operation. The family was content to focus its efforts in the carousel building, which by now contained a bumper car ride and a growing collection of kiddie rides.

As America entered World War II, rationing and materials shortages made things difficult for Ocean City, although the family managed to open a new hotel in 1944, the Inlet Lodge, which continues to operate. With its oceanfront location, Trimper's had to take precautions against enemy attack and, as a result, illuminated the park with ten-watt light bulbs shielded inside tin cans.

Nineteen fifty-two was a critical year for the long-term future of Trimper's as Granville Trimper, nephew of Daniel Trimper Jr., joined the amusement park. For much of his youth, Granville assisted his father Granville Sr. with his carnival operation. At the age of ten, he was given responsibility for a kiddie car ride, setting it up, taking it down, and operating it. By the age of twelve, he says, "I wanted something of my own." His father took him to the bank to get a $5,000 loan to purchase his own Ferris wheel from the Eli Bridge Company. Again he was responsible for setting it up and taking it down. "I was a big kid at twelve," he recalls.

In 1952, however, not only did Granville's father pass away, but the carnival's winter quarters was destroyed by fire, taking several rides. At that point, Granville decided to put down roots at the amusement park and set up his Ferris wheel next to Inlet Lodge where it was soon joined by other large spinning rides such as the Tilt-A-Whirl, the Merry Mixer, and the Spitfire.

The Ferris wheel remains a beloved attraction at the park. It has survived being blown over in two storms, and to this day, the park removes four seats each night to lessen the possibility of wind damage. For years, Granville would offer $100 to anyone who could pick up the wheel's main axle, something the strapping man could do with ease.

By the early 1950s, the carousel was showing its age. As a result, the Trimper family asked a local housepainter to freshen up the ride. Since he was unfamiliar with painting animals, he used a children's picture book as a guide. Upon completion, the Trimpers noticed that the formerly green dragon was bright red. Apparently, the book didn't have a picture of a dragon, so the painter used a picture of a lobster on a nearby restaurant for inspiration. The dragon was soon repainted.

By the end of the fifties, although the last remnants of Daniel Trimper's original hotels were demolished, Ocean City had become one of the most popular resorts on the Eastern seaboard with the 1952 completion of the Bay Bridge making access to Baltimore and Washington even easier.

By now Daniel Trimper's old Windsor Theater was declining in popularity. Granville, who had taken on increasing responsibility, closed it and converted the theater into a night club and then a roller rink. In 1961, he took a trip to Glen Echo Park, outside Washington, D.C., and was intrigued by that park's haunted house ride.

Upon returning to Ocean City, he got in contact with Bill Tracy, one of the leading attraction designers of the era to develop a similar ride for Trimper's. In February 1962 construction began to convert the former theater into the Haunted House. Its spooky facade made an immediate impression on the bustling boardwalk and it has been a favorite attraction ever since.

Daniel Trimper Jr. died in 1965 at the age of seventy-nine, and control of the growing amusement park passed into the hands of cousins Granville and Daniel Trimper III. But while one generation faded away, the next generation entered the business when Granville's son, fifteen-year-old Douglas, purchased a Corvette kiddie ride to operate at the park.

The Haunted House first opened in the former theater building in 1962. It underwent a major expansion in 1988.

Getting Bigger and Better

The new generation brought a renewed vigor to the park and by the end of the 1960s a major overhaul of the operation was launched in response to increasing crowds and the addition of amusement rides on the nearby Ocean City Pier. The expansive carousel building was remodeled in 1967, and the next few seasons focused on developing the parking lot behind the carousel building into a ride area. In 1969, five rides, representing some of the most modern of the time, made their debuts. Three, the Matterhorn, the Himalaya, and the Olympic Bobs, were flashy rides where cars traveled over a circular undulating track at a high rate of speed, accompanied by lights and music. Also added were the Turbo, a short-lived Ferris-wheel-type ride, and the Toboggan, a compact roller coaster. Riders start out on the Toboggan by being hauled straight up the inside of a 45-foot-tall tower. The cars then spiral downward around the tower before negotiating a series of dips on its 450-foot-long track.

In 1971, Bill Tracy returned to build the Pirate's Cove, a walk-through attraction featuring a variety of pirate-themed obstacles that visitors must negotiate. It was soon followed by additional outdoor expansion including rides such as the Zipper, the Rotor, the Sky Diver, electric go-carts, the Yo Yo swing ride, and the Aladdin's Lamp, a large fun house.

By the mid-seventies, Trimper's was able to fill out its holdings with the purchase of Melvin Amusements, a small five-ride amusement park

Trimper's started adding rides in the area behind the carousel building in the late 1960s.

that shared the block. Dating back to the late 1950s, the park featured several spinning rides, the Mirror Maze walk-through, and the Wild Mouse roller coaster. One of the most popular rides of its era, the Wild Mouse was erected in the late 1950s and offered sharp turns rather than drops to provide its thrills. It stood approximately 35 feet tall and was 1,000 feet long.

Trimper's moved quickly to integrate the park into its existing operation. The wood track Wild Mouse was jacked up on rollers and moved 70 feet in one piece to create room for more rides. Also, the Mirror Maze was relocated and a couple of the spinning rides removed.

A New Wave

In 1980, Daniel III retired, leaving Granville in control of the operation. The highlight that year was the completion of a multiyear restoration of the carousel. Siblings John and Maria Bilous were hired to restore the ride. Working on two animals at a time so that the carousel could remain in operation, the pair carefully removed years of grime and paint that had accumulated on each figure to reveal its original colors.

Given the unique nature of the project, the Bilouses faced numerous challenges in finding the right way to restore the ride. The first animal fell apart when it was dipped in paint remover, which also dissolved the glue. They then settled on a water-soluble paint thinner and a pressure hose, which struck the proper balance between removing unwanted paint and protecting the animals.

Once the animals were complete, all of the scenery panels were given the same treatment, and a thick accumulation of green paint was removed from the platform floor to reveal the original wood. When the pair completed the carousel, they then went to work on the antique kiddie rides, including the merry-go-round and the Ferris wheel, to restore the original paint jobs. The most dramatic discovery, however, was the elaborate hand-painted scenes that were uncovered on each of the kiddie whip's cars.

The work continues to this day. Maria Bilous (now Schlick) now works for Trimper's full-time as the carousel curator, constantly working to ensure the carousel remains in pristine condition. Several animals are removed annually on a rotating basis for a complete overhaul.

With the park's oldest ride restored, Granville turned his attention to other major projects. In 1983, he added Inlet Village, a $1.5 million shopping center next to the amusement park featuring fourteen shops and restaurants; but the addition of Inlet Village did not mean that the amusement park was being ignored. A water slide was constructed, and rides such as the Tank Battle and the Sky Wheel, a double Ferris wheel, were added.

The 1986 construction of the Tidal Wave roller coaster was Trimper's largest and most successful expansion.

In 1986, the skyline of Trimper's Rides and Amusements was forever changed with the largest project in park history. With crowds demanding larger and more thrilling rides, Trimper's was challenged to come up with an attraction that combined the maximum amount of thrills into a minimum amount of space—in Trimper's case, just 306 linear feet. They found such a ride with Vekoma, a Dutch ride manufacturer, and their then new Boomerang roller coaster. On the ride, the train is hauled backward up a 125-foot-tall incline. It is then released and travels back through the station into a twisting "Boomerang" that flips riders upside down two times and then through a vertical loop before traveling up another 125-foot-tall incline. The train then reverses and goes through everything again backward. In all, riders are turned upside down six times along just 875 feet of track. Named the Tidal Wave, it was just the second ride of its kind in North America. To clear space for the Tidal Wave, Trimper's retired the Wild Mouse along with the Olympic Bobs and the Round Up, rides which were part of the Melvin Amusements purchase. The $1.3 million gamble paid off with the Tidal Wave becoming the most profitable investment the park ever made.

With Trimper's oldest and newest rides firmly entrenched, in 1988 the family turned their attention to another one of their classic attractions. Playland, a nearby amusement park, had closed several years earlier and was liquidating its rides. Trimper's purchased its dark ride and used it to launch a major reconstruction and expansion of the Haunted House. A new two-level structure was built to accommodate both several new scenes and a section of track that came out of the building giving riders a view of the boardwalk. Rather than hiring a manufacturer to do the work, it was a true family project with everyone pitching in and Granville supervising. As part of the project, the Mirror Maze also was given a new building.

After a decade under Granville's guidance, Trimper's Rides and Amusements had grown about as much as it could. There just was not any more room. As a result the 1990s were characterized by continuous upgrades of the park's ride lineup. The Wipeout, a high-speed spinning ride, replaced the Yo Yo swing ride in 1992. It was tucked under one of the Tidal Wave loops, where it was joined by a new kiddie train ride. Also that year, Marty's Playland, a nearby arcade operation was purchased; and the waterslide was closed in the face of declining popularity.

The Avalanche, another compact thriller, debuted in 1996; and the 1999 season saw the Ghost Hole, a gravity-powered dark ride sold to New York's Coney Island and replaced by the Inverter, a flipping ride for the heartiest of stomachs. By the end of that season, the Sky Wheel gave its last rides.

With the dawn of the twenty-first century, Trimper's sought to maintain a balance between family rides and thrill rides. In 2001, the Slingshot, a 110-foot-tall tower ride was added along with the spinning tea cups; and the Rockin' Tug, another family ride, debuted in 2003.

Trimper's has continued to mix thrill rides with family rides as it has grown.

Crowds were continuing to grow, and in 2005 the family decided to add more room to the thriving operation by converting a miniature golf course into a new ride area. Granville's original Ferris wheel was moved to the parcel where it was joined by the Freak Out, an intense thrill ride. In 2006, four new family rides were added including the Flying Tigers in the main ride area. Rides in the new area included two new kiddie rides and the Wacky Worm, a 13-foot-tall, 450-foot-long roller coaster for the whole family.

Trimper's Rides and Amusements Today

It's hard to imagine Ocean City without Trimper's Rides and Amusements. For over a century, it has anchored this beachside community and has played a key role in its growth into a major resort. Today visitors find an action-packed amusement park with over forty rides including the classic carousel, three roller coasters, the Haunted House dark ride, and five walk-through attractions, all packed in an area slightly larger than a city block.

The large carousel building opens onto the boardwalk. A number of shops, concessions, and the Haunted House dark ride all front the boardwalk. Entering the building, visitors come across the heart and soul of Trimper's Rides and Amusements, the antique carousel. A dozen lovingly maintained kiddie rides, several dating back nearly ninety years, surround the carousel, including the whip with its beautiful hand-painted scenes. Also found in the building are the bumper car ride and several games.

Directly behind the building is the largest of Trimper's three outdoor ride areas. Featured here are the Tidal Wave and the Toboggan roller coasters; thrill rides such as the Himalaya, the Wipeout, and the Merry Mixer; family rides including the Flying Tigers, the Balloons, and the Rockin' Tug, as well as the Aladdin's Lamp, the Pirate Ship, and the Raiders walk-through attractions.

Turning left out of the back of the building, across South 1st Street, one comes across the ride area featuring many of the larger, high-speed rides including the Slingshot tower, the Matterhorn, the Inverter, the Avalanche, and the Zipper.

Turning right out of the back of the building leads to the newer ride area, across South Division Street. Although most of the rides are geared toward families including the Ferris wheel and the Wacky Worm roller coaster, it is also home to the Freak Out thrill ride.

Jolly Roger at the Pier

OPENED 1907

ALTHOUGH ONLY TWO DECADES OLD, THE GIANT FERRIS WHEEL AT JOLLY Roger at the Pier has become one of Ocean City's most memorable landmarks. Towering more than ten stories above the beach, it calls visitors to the action-packed southern tip of the boardwalk. At night its dazzling lights add to the magical atmosphere of the boardwalk; but although the wheel is relatively new, its home, Ocean City's pier, has been part of the seaside resort for more than a century.

Growing with the Town

Since it was founded in 1875, Ocean City gradually grew into a favorite vacation destination for the residents of the mid-Atlantic. In 1902, local businessmen laid out the town's first boardwalk, a temporary assemblage of planks that was taken in at high tide and in the winter. Although entertainment offerings had been increasing, they were still limited. As a result, in 1904, a local entrepreneur, William Preston Laws, first proposed the idea of building a recreational pier at the emerging resort.

He soon formed a group that organized the Ocean City Pier and Improvement Company, led by William Taylor, who was charged with building the pier. In 1907, Ocean City's pier was ready for visitors. In those days before the permanent boardwalk was erected, the entrance to the pier stood at least 5 feet above the walk.

Along the boardwalk, visitors were greeted by a large white wood frame building with a rounded roof and arched windows built on pilings over the

Jolly Roger at the Pier
2901 Coastal Highway
Ocean City, Maryland 21842
410-289-3477
info@jollyrogerpark.com
www.jollyrogerpark.com

beach. At the time the beach was narrow enough that part of the building was over the surf. A large front porch overlooked the boardwalk and inside people could enjoy a dance pavilion, a movie theater, bowling, billiards, and a restaurant.

Behind the main building, the pier extended several hundred feet into the ocean. Here, one could rent fishing equipment or engage in trap shooting competitions. Another building at the end featured a roller rink.

The pier immediately emerged as one of the community's top attractions, becoming a pleasant place to while away a summer evening. In 1918, an accumulation of winter ice and snow caused the pier to collapse, but it didn't slow down the owners, who had it ready for visitors the next summer.

The winter collapse paled in comparison, however, to its next challenge. At 7:30 A.M. on December 29, 1925, a fire started in the Eastern Shore Gas and Electric Company plant two blocks from the pier. Smoke could be seen 10 miles away and with a stiff northwest wind, the fire quickly spread, aided by cold weather that froze fire hydrants. As a result, fire fighters had to cut holes in the ice in the bay and pump the water three blocks across the island. The town women even had to sit on the hoses to keep them from twisting. By the end of the day, three blocks of the town had been leveled. Four hotels including the Atlantic and the

Ocean City's pier originally featured this building on the boardwalk. It was destroyed in the 1925 fire.

LOCATION

Jolly Roger at the Pier is located at the southern tip of Ocean City, along the boardwalk between Worcester and Wicomico Streets. From U.S. Route 50, cross the H. Kelly Memorial Bridge over Sinepuxent Bay. Turn right on Philadelphia Avenue to South First Street. Look for the giant Ferris wheel.

Pay parking is available at the municipal lot next to the pier.

OPERATING SCHEDULE

Jolly Roger at the Pier is open from 2 P.M. to midnight daily from Memorial Day weekend through Labor Day.

ADMISSION

Admission to the pier is free with a choice of paying by the ride or buying a one price wristband. Visitors can purchase points on a Jolly Roger Passport to Fun card for approximately 60 cents each with rides taking between four and five and a half points. Points are also good for the games.

The pay-one-price wristband costs under $20 and permits visitors to enjoy all rides and attractions.

Points and wristbands purchased at Jolly Roger at the Pier can also be used at Jolly Roger Amusement Park.

Admission to the fishing pier at the end of Jolly Roger at the Pier costs extra.

FOOD

There are six food stands located at Jolly Roger at the Pier. Four of the stands are located along the boardwalk, and two are on the pier itself. Don't miss Thrashers along the boardwalk. Occupying the same location since the building was erected in 1929, Thrasher's french fries are a boardwalk tradition. The fresh potatoes are served hot out of the fryer and are often topped by malt vinegar. But don't bother asking for ketchup. They don't have it.

Next to Thrashers is Boog's Barbecue. Named after legendary Baltimore Orioles baseball player Boog Powell, the stand is known for its pork barbecue.

On the pier, the major food stand is the Pier Café featuring hot dogs, burgers, subs, and chicken fingers.

Don't miss the variety of food concessions located along the boardwalk. Highlights include Dolle's Candyland, which has been selling saltwater taffy and other treats since 1910; Dumser's Dairyland, which has been serving ice cream on the boardwalk since 1939; the Dough Roller for pizza and pancakes; and Phillips Restaurants, known for their seafood.

FOR CHILDREN

Jolly Roger at the Pier features a number of family rides including the Ferris wheel, the double-deck merry-go-round, and several others.

(continued on page 68)

VISITING (continued from page 67)

SPECIAL FEATURES

Don't miss the giant Ferris wheel. Towering over 100 feet above the beach, it's a great way to take in the view of the town.

TIME REQUIRED

Although the pier can be experienced in about two hours, visitors should plan to spend the day in Ocean City and enjoy the beach and all of the boardwalk attractions.

TOURING TIPS

To avoid crowds, visit the park during the afternoon, particularly on weekdays.

Admission plans purchased at Jolly Roger at the Pier can also be used at Jolly Roger Park. So if you plan to visit both, plan accordingly to get the most for your money.

Seaside, the largest in town, were gone. Two blocks of the boardwalk where wiped out including Dolle's Candyland, the Casino Theater, a carousel, and an assortment of concessions. The pier was reduced to some charred pilings sticking out of the water.

Its tenants, including a ladies' ready-to-wear shop, a bowling alley, a soda fountain, and a pool hall, lost everything. The Jester family, which operated a souvenir stand and lunchroom at the pier and later owned a large fun house on the boardwalk, saved only a bag of green peanuts, but even that was soon stolen.

Starting Anew

For more than a year, the burned-out pier languished as various proposals were made for reconstructing the facility. Finally, in 1927, the Sinepuxent Pier and Improvement Company was incorporated to rebuild the pier. The company obtained a new franchise from the city, sold shares to finance the project, and named Clarence Whealton, a lawyer from nearby Salisbury, as president.

By the spring of 1929, the new 700-foot-long pier was complete. Strollers along the boardwalk were greeted by a new two-story building featuring stores and food concessions on the first floor and a ballroom on the second. Among the first-floor concessions was Thrashers, which remains today as an Ocean City institution, selling over a million pounds of its famous french fries annually.

The timing for the new ballroom was perfect as the big band era was hitting its peak. For much of the 1930s, the pier swung to the sounds of major bands led by Glenn Miller, Jimmy Dorsey, Benny Goodman, and others.

Business at the pier continued to be solid through the 1940s, but by the 1950s, times were changing. Ballroom dancing was declining in popularity and the big bands stopped coming to town. As a result, the ballroom was pressed into service as a convention hall and teen center, but traffic had decreased, hurting all of the business at the pier. It appeared the pier's best days were behind it.

In 1957, area business leaders announced plans to replace the aging facility with an all new 600-foot-long, 160-foot-wide three-level pier. Financed by another stock sale, the proposed attractions included a bathhouse, a fishing balcony, a convention hall, a theater, concessions, a ballroom, a restaurant, and even a heliport and broadcasting studio.

The costly proposal went nowhere and control of the pier passed to a new company that developed another plan to add amusement park rides and attractions to the pier. In a special referendum, town voters defeated the proposal, objecting to the honky-tonk atmosphere intruding on the town's beaches.

Despite the defeat, the town eventually permitted Buster Gordon to set up about a dozen rides on the pier in the mid-1960s. Although they were primarily carnival-type spinning rides such as the Loop-O-Plane, the Paratrooper, the Scrambler, the Trabant and a fun house, they generated new traffic at the aging facility.

Amusement rides first appeared on the pier in the 1960s.

A New Life

In 1974, Ocean City native Charles Jenkins, resort investor and owner of the nearby Jolly Roger Amusement Park, purchased all shares in the pier company. He launched a $1.5 million renovation of the pier and brought in new concessions and amusements operated by Dick Marchant, a well-known ride broker. Among the attractions ready for the 1975 season was Morbid Manor, a large walk-through haunted house attraction. It quickly became an Ocean City landmark. One of its unique features was a séance room where visitors would sit around a table and find it rising in the air while spinning.

Also opening in 1975 was the pier's first roller coaster, the City Jet. Standing 36 feet high with a compact 1,350-foot-long layout, it was the perfect ride for the confined pier. The improvements brought new life to the facility and in 1978, the city gave Jenkins a fifty-year lease. That year, the boardwalk building took on a new life when a Ripley's Believe It or Not! Museum opened on the second floor.

Unfortunately, in February 1979, ice jams resulting from cold winter weather destroyed 140 feet at the end of the pier used by fishermen. Although the city pressed Jenkins to rebuild the damaged portion, he argued that it did not need to be rebuilt as the construction of a stone jetty in 1933 changed ocean currents—meaning that fishing would not be enhanced by the longer pier. In the end, difficulty in obtaining permits from the Army Corps of Engineers and scarcity of the 55-foot-long pilings needed for the project resolved the dispute and the pier remained in its shortened state.

The facility's emerging ride lineup was drastically altered in 1981 when the lease for the ride operations was purchased from Marchant by Donnie Degeller, a carnival operator. The City Jet and several other rides were removed and nine new ones were added including spinning rides such as the Waltzer, an intense spinner

Morbid Manor was the pier's most famous attraction from 1975 until it burned down in 1995.

The Giant Wheel has become one of Ocean City's most recognizable icons.

from England; the Himalaya; and the Zyclon, a compact steel roller coaster. In addition, two dozen games were added. After a couple of seasons, the Zyclon was replaced by the Flitzer, a 25-foot-high, 1,200-foot-long twisting steel track roller coaster from Zierer of Germany.

Five years later, when Degeller's lease expired, Jenkins decided to bring the pier's ride operations under his umbrella. As a result, Jenkins went ride shopping, visiting manufacturers in Germany, Italy, and Switzerland. Among the rides he brought home to populate the pier were a 1001 Nights, a Music Express, an Enterprise, and a 110-foot-tall Ferris wheel with twenty-four gondolas. Adorned with an elaborate light package, the Ferris wheel instantly became one of Ocean City's most recognizable landmarks.

Jenkins followed up in 1987 by adding a water park to the end of the pier featuring nine waterslides, including one of world's tallest speed slides, along with body flumes, a shotgun slide, and a lazy river. Not much changed at the pier for the next several years. Rides would be rotated out and replaced by others to keep things fresh including the high speed Crazy Dance, which debuted in 1995. Some anchors such as the Ferris wheel and Morbid Manor, however, remained steadfast.

That was changed on November 5, 1995, when a fire destroyed Morbid Manor; but Jenkins took the loss as an opportunity to refresh the

Installed in 2006, the Morbid Manor II dark ride is a tribute to the original Morbid Manor.

entire pier. The waterslides were moved to sister park Jolly Roger, where they became part of its Splash Mountain water park. New decking was added to much of the pier and four new rides were acquired—the Balloon Ride; a double-deck Venetian merry-go-round from Italy; the Ghost, a new dark ride; and a new roller coaster, the Looping Star. Manufactured by Pinfari, the well-known Italian manufacturer of compact steel roller coasters, the Looping Star stands 36 feet tall and packs in a vertical loop on its 1,200-foot-long course.

The next major change at the pier occurred in 2001 when the Rock 'n Rapids appeared. A compact log flume from Reverchon of France, it packed two drops of 30 and 40 feet along its 750-foot-long trough. After three years, the flume gave way to other rides.

Also in 2001, an old favorite returned when Ripley's Entertainment Incorporated opened a new Believe It or Not! Museum. The original museum had closed in 1984 and in the interim the space had been used as a laser tag attraction. Located on the 10,000-square-foot second level, the new Ripley's features more than 500 one-of-a-kind curiosities from around the world, including dinosaur artifacts, shrunken heads, torture chamber devices, an autopsy table, a 42-foot roller coaster model, and a meteorite from Mars. To get the attention of boardwalk strollers, Ripley's installed a 50-foot-long animated shark crashing out of the front of the building. It became an instant boardwalk landmark, and the museum exceeded projections its first season.

Most recently, the park officially changed its name to Jolly Roger at the Pier, to tie it in with its nearby sister park, Jolly Roger Amusement Park. To celebrate the name change, a new dark ride, named Morbid Manor II in honor of the departed Morbid Manor, opened in 2006, replacing the Ghost. The new dark ride is itself a piece of history, originally being built as a portable attraction in the mid-1970s. Also joining the lineup was the Slingshot, a bungee-style attraction that flings riders into the sky.

Jolly Roger at the Pier Today

Jolly Roger at the Pier has become a century-old fixture on Ocean City's bustling boardwalk. With its towering Ferris wheel and imposing board-walk side building, complete with a shark sticking out of the front, it is not difficult to locate the pier. The two-story building is home to several food, merchandise, and games concessions including the legendary Thrasher's french fry stand and the Ripley's Believe It or Not! Museum. A passageway lined with games through the building provides access to the heart of the pier. Along the pier, visitors will find the Sling Shot, the Morbid Manor II, and a number of spinning rides to the left, and the bumper cars, Ferris wheel, and the Looping Star roller coaster to the right. The double-deck merry-go-round anchors a central location in the back of the pier, where visitors can access the fishing pier section.

Funland

OPENED 1939

A DAY IN THE LIFE OF FUNLAND REFLECTS THE PACE OF THIS SEASIDE resort town. When the town awakens on a sleepy summer morning and visitors head to the beach, Funland slowly comes to life as its arcade and games open to capture the occasional passerby on the boardwalk. When the sun grows high in the sky, the rides come to life as families start to look for diversions beyond the beach. By early evening, as the lure of the beach wears off, the pace at Funland picks up when the Haunted Mansion, its most popular attraction, starts to welcome visitors. Once the sun goes down, Funland is at its peak. The lights of the rides and wall-to-wall crowds of families create an electric atmosphere that mirrors the throngs strolling the boardwalk. Then in the wee hours, Funland joins the rest of the town in settling down for the night, only to repeat that cycle the next day.

Spill the Milk

In 1938, Jack Dentino arrived in the beachside community of Rehoboth Beach, Delaware. Having visited Wildwood, New Jersey, frequently in the past, he sought to bring some of the excitement of that storied boardwalk to the much quieter town. Dentino was able to secure a location at the corner of Delaware Avenue and the boardwalk, just south of the heart of town. In the spring of 1939, he opened a Spill the Milk game on the site, a classic game in which players try to knock over a pyramid of six wooden milk bottles with a baseball. Customers paid a

Funland
6 Delaware Avenue
Rehoboth Beach, DE 19971
302-227-1921
funland@funlandrehoboth.com
www.funlandrehoboth.com

nickel for three tries. Behind the game, he built a room where he slept on a cot during the summer.

Dentino quickly expanded his operation by adding batting cages, a shooting gallery, and miniature golf. He named the operation the Sports Center, reflecting the nature of the attractions.

As World War II ended, the corner where Dentino started with the Spill the Milk game became home to a new boardwalk landmark—a two-story frame building distinguished by a corner tower. It sat atop a substantial foundation of cement and steel, which Dentino dug deep into the ground using a mule-drawn shovel.

By the 1950s, the postwar baby boom brought a new generation of visitors to Rehoboth Beach, and Dentino responded by adding kiddie rides. The first rides added were typical kiddie rides of the era, a fire engine and a boat ride purchased from the Pinto Brothers Company of Coney Island, New York, a kiddie merry-go-round, a small whip, a home-made Ferris wheel, and a unique park-built turnpike ride that used Vespa scooters to carry riders through the course. Dentino even managed to squeeze a miniature train and a bumper car ride into the 35,000-square-foot site. By 1956, the Sports Center featured eleven rides, two games, a shooting gallery, miniature golf, and basketball.

In 1959, Dentino added a merry-go-round ride, featuring aluminum horses, purchased from the Allan Herschell Company, which in the 1950s was the world's largest ride manufacturer. The Sports Center followed

Rides first appeared at Funland in the 1950s when it was known as the Sports Center.

up the successful debut of the merry-go-round in 1960 with the addition of the helicopter ride. Also built by Allan Herschell, it was one of the most popular rides of the era, in which riders in helicopter-shaped vehicles controlled their height by moving a bar back and forth. Versions of the ride continue to be a staple in amusement parks around the world.

By the early 1960s, Rehoboth Beach was a summer institution. People thronged to the boardwalk and to Dentino's operation, but he was tiring of the grind and was looking to sell.

In August of 1961, the Fasnacht family traveled from Hershey, Pennsylvania, for a vacation at the beach. The Fasnachts had purchased Willow Mill Park, a popular picnic-oriented amusement park outside Harrisburg, Pennsylvania, in 1956 and were quite enamored with the amusement industry.

Naturally, they were interested in visiting the Sports Center to check out the operation. Al Fasnacht was intrigued with the helicopter ride, thinking it would be a great addition at Willow Mill. He started to speak to the operator, but discovered he was reluctant to talk. As Fasnacht recalls, "The operator told me the boss does not like them talking to customers, and pointed out Dentino to me." Fasnacht introduced himself to the park owner and the first thing out of his mouth was "Hello," followed by the question, "Do you want to buy this place?"

"My first thought was, 'We have one headache, we don't need another,'" but he also liked Rehoboth Beach's family-oriented atmosphere and the idea of living at the beach. When he brought up the idea to his father, Allen, his first reaction was "We don't need another headache"; but the next day, he had a change of heart and the family returned to Delaware to take a closer look at the Sports Center. Later that fall, the parties met in Wilmington, Delaware, at Dentino's "additors" as he liked to call auditors, to start negotiations. With an agreement nearly complete, Dentino wanted to finalize the deal on March 1, but the Fasnachts preferred April 1. As a compromise, the parties decided to split the difference. On March 15, 1962, the Sports Center would belong to the Fasnachts.

An Ill Wind Blows

By early March, the Fasnacht family was making the final preparations to take control of the Sports Center. Allen and Sis, his wife, would move to Rehoboth Beach for the summer and run that park, while their sons, Al and Don, would continue to run Willow Mill Park.

As they were making preparations, however, a storm was brewing along the North Carolina coast. By the time it reached Delaware on March 5, it was generating northeasterly winds of 80 miles per hour, the most powerful storm to hit the state in more than fifty years. Over the course of three days, it pounded the shore with waves up to 40 feet tall.

 **VISITING**

FUNLAND

LOCATION

Funland is located on Rehoboth Beach's boardwalk at Delaware Avenue. From the south, take U.S. Route 1 to U.S. Route 1B, which merges into Rehoboth Avenue (U.S. Route 1A). From the north, take U.S. Route 1 to Rehoboth Avenue (U.S. Route 1A). Follow Rehoboth Avenue to First Street. After turning right on First Street, go south two blocks to Delaware Avenue. Turn left on Delaware and the park will be on your right at the ocean. Street parking is available in the neighborhood, although it's in short supply on summer weekends.

OPERATING SCHEDULE

Funland kicks off the season each year on Mother's Day weekend, opening weekends at 1 P.M. through the month of May. Closing time is dependent on crowds and weather, but is typically 11 P.M. on Saturdays and 9 P.M. on Sundays.

Daily operation starts the first week of June and runs through Labor Day. The arcade and selected games open at 10 A.M., rides at 1 P.M., and the Haunted Mansion at 6:30 P.M. The rides typically close at 11 P.M., although closing time is dependent on weather and crowd conditions.

Funland is also open evenings the week after Labor Day from 7 to 9 P.M. and the weekend after Labor Day with the arcade and games opening at 10 A.M. and the rides at 1 P.M.

ADMISSION

Admission to Funland is free with rides available on a pay-as-you-go basis. Tickets cost about 30 cents each and rides take between one and five tickets. Discount ticket books are available.

FOOD

Funland has no on-site food service facilities, preferring to let customers enjoy the wealth of offerings along the boardwalk and in town. Notable outlets include Dolle's Salt Water Taffy, a boardwalk institution since 1927, which sells 100,000 pounds of candy every summer; Thrashers, known for its french fries; Grotto Pizza, considered the best in Delaware; and Gus and Gus Place, which has been serving hamburgers, hot dogs, gyros, and french fries along the boardwalk for over fifty years.

FOR CHILDREN

All of Funland is geared to families and their children. The park has eight rides and a play area especially for kids. The majority of the remaining ten rides can be enjoyed by most members of the family.

SPECIAL FEATURES

Funland's Haunted Mansion is one of the best dark rides around. Few dark rides have the attention to detail and extensive scenes that the Haunted Mansion does. Its one-of-a-kind transportation system is another bonus.

(continued on page 78)

VISITING (continued from page 77)

FUNLAND, REHOBOTH BEACH

Funland takes great pride in the fact that it tries to target its games toward its family-oriented clientele with reasonable prices and relatively easy-to-win games.

TIME REQUIRED

To fully experience Funland, two hours should be sufficient, although families with smaller children will likely want to spend more time. Visitors should plan, however, to spend the day in Rehoboth Beach and enjoy the beach and all of the boardwalk attractions.

TOURING TIPS

Two-thirds of Funland is under roof, so don't let inclement weather ruin your plans.

The Haunted Mansion is only open in the evening, so if you want to enjoy that ride, plan accordingly.

When the storm passed, the Fasnachts made a beeline to town to see how the Sports Center held up. Initially, they were encouraged as damage in the town was minimal. "You saw no sign of the storm until you reached the boardwalk," remembers Al Fasnacht. "Then it was utter destruction." The mile-long boardwalk was destroyed; several town landmarks, such as the Henlopen and the Atlantic Sands hotels and Dolle's candy shop, saw their waterfront facades washed into the ocean; and pretty much every other beachfront building was destroyed.

The Sports Center was severely damaged. Many of the park's buildings had been built directly on the ground, not on pilings; and as the storm washed out the sand underneath, the buildings collapsed. Several I-beams were bent by concrete slabs and heavy timber being hurled by the pounding surf like battering rams. All of the doors and most of floorboards were blown or washed away. The bumper car ride's floor had completely collapsed; and the cars were washed out on the beach and buried, with only their power poles visible. To top it off, the park was filled with tons of sand.

One structure that did escape serious damage was Dentino's corner building with its concrete and steel foundation, although it did sink 19 inches. Because of this, the building became something of a legend. For several years it was used by the Bethlehem Steel Company in promotional materials touting the benefits of reinforced-steel construction.

"It was utter desolation," Al Fasnacht recalls. "We wondered what we had gotten ourselves into." Although Dentino offered to let the family out of the deal, the Fasnachts took the plunge and closed on the purchase, aided by a $50,000 reduction in the purchase price. "I don't think we ever doubted that we made the right decision."

As devastating as the storm was, some good came out of it. Playland, a similar amusement park next door, had been a strong competitor for several years; so much so that Dentino had purchased a house behind the property to prevent it from expanding. But the storm washed away Playland's main building, which contained most of its kiddie rides, and the park was never rebuilt. Rehoboth Beach belonged to Funland.

Needless to say the Fasnachts had their work cut out for them, but they enthusiastically plunged into the challenge. Remnants of the park were salvaged from the beach; sand was removed from the property; and the corner building was jacked up to its original height. In addition, substantial buildings of cement and steel replaced their wooden predecessors. Although most rides were able to be repaired, the family removed five of them including the turnpike, the kiddie Ferris wheel, and the whip, because they did not fit with their plans for the park. By Memorial Day, 1962, just ten weeks after the storm, the newly named Funland was ready for customers.

Funland struggled that first season. Since the boardwalk had not yet been re-erected, business was slow; but in the end, the family managed to make a small profit. Then in the fall, another storm roared though town blowing off the roof of the newly built merry-go-round building.

Funland was extensively damaged by a storm in March 1962 just ten days before the Fasnacht family was slated to purchase the facility. FUNLAND

Despite this minor setback, Funland had come back from the devastation and was ready to grow. In 1963, the park added the Crazy Dazy, a spinning teacup ride. As business increased, the family sold Willow Mill Park in 1968, allowing Al and Don to come to Rehoboth Beach to work side by side with their parents. Today, over thirty members of the Fasnacht family work at Funland.

The park continued to grow throughout the 1970s. In 1975 a Paratrooper ride replaced the train ride, and the following season a new building was erected on an adjoining 15,000-square-foot parcel of land that the family has assembled over the previous few years. It housed a new bumper car ride and other attractions including the relocated Crazy Dazy. A spinning Trabant ride was acquired from Dorney Park, Allentown, Pennsylvania, in 1978, a year in which work started on the park's most ambitious project ever.

A Haunting Addition

For several years Funland had wanted to add a dark ride, and the new building included a second story to accommodate such an attraction. Initially, they approached the Pretzel Ride Company, one of the industry's leading dark ride manufacturers, about building the ride; but they could not come up with a feasible concept. The park also considered purchasing an existing Haunted House dark ride from the shuttered West View Park in Pittsburgh, Pennsylvania, but nixed that idea when they heard a story of how one of the cars once broke loose from the track and rolled down the midway.

Funland then heard about a trailer-mounted dark ride built by Venture Ride Manufacturing of Greer, South Carolina. It utilized a unique transport system that suspended the cars underneath an overhead rail. The park thought such a concept would be the prefect way to get riders from the ground level loading station to the heart of the ride on the second floor above the bumper cars.

Adapting a little-used technology in a unique environment, however, presented an entirely new set of challenges to Funland. A special braking system had to be custom designed, the sections to get the cars up to and down from the second floor needed to be modified, special loading mechanisms had to be created, and the motors had to be adapted to the unique demands of the ride's location.

Once the challenges of the system were worked out, work on the scenes began. Leading the effort was Jim Melonic from Fantasies and Dreams—a successor to the Amusement Display Company that was owned by Bill Tracy, the leading manufacturer of dark ride stunts and ride theming in the 1960s. Melonic provided the ride's facade, stunts, and sets.

Added in 1980, the Haunted Mansion is Funland's most popular attraction.

In 1980, after over two years of work, the Haunted Mansion opened
to eager throngs. Since that time, it has become a boardwalk institution
and one of the best traditional dark rides in the industry. With scenes
around every corner and sections that travel above the park and over-
look the boardwalk, visitors have to ride it several times just to take it all
in. Funland, considering the Haunted Mansion to be a work in progress,
is always working to enhance the experience.

"It was something we dreamed about, planned and put together ourselves. And we encountered and overcame problems that we never
dreamed we'd have," Al Fasnacht told *Fun World* magazine about the
experience of creating the Haunted House.

Throughout the 1980s, Funland worked to improve its ride lineup. In
1983, the park replaced the Trabant with the unique Wagon Wheeler.
One of only three rides of its kind, the Wagon Wheeler featured cars
that riders rocked back and forth, trying to get them to turn in a complete loop.

The Gravitron, a spinning ride that creates the sensation of weight-
lessness, appeared in 1985 followed by a play area for the kids in 1987.
The mini Himalaya was added from Venture Rides in 1989, the same
year that Allen Fasnacht passed away at the age of eighty-one. Nineteen
ninety saw the debut of Funland's biggest ride, the Sea Dragon, a large
swinging ship. Installing the ride in the cramped amusement park turned
out to be quite a challenge. It was squeezed into a tight space in the back

of the park and Funland did not truly know if the swinging contraption would actually fit until it was operated the first time. It turns out it did, missing a neighboring building by just 13 inches.

With little room left to expand, the park's focus was placed on upgrading the facilities. A new boardwalk facade was added, and Dentino's cor-

Top: The unique Wagon Wheeler operated at Funland from 1983 to 1995. Bottom: Most of Funland's kiddie rides are located under cover. FUNLAND

ner building was replaced with a new structure. A Chaos spinning ride replaced the Wagon Wheeler in 1996, and a major upgrade of the merry-go-round was undertaken in 2000 in honor of Sis Fasnacht who passed away in 1998 at the age of ninety-one. Since opening at the park in 1959 and surviving the storm in 1962 the ride had become dated in appearance. As a result Funland sent it to Chance Rides of Wichita, Kansas, the world's largest merry-go-round manufacturer, for the installation of scenery panels based on classic Dentzel carousels from the early twentieth century.

As a new century dawned, upgrades were a constant theme. Although many of the classics remained, newer rides were added such as a kiddie truck ride in 2001 and the Freefall, which opened in 2004.

Replacing the kiddie-oriented Frog Hopper tower ride, which opened in 1999, the Freefall was manufactured by the Italian firm Moser Rides. The 21-foot-tall tower can accommodate the entire family with its dropping, bouncing motions. Funland had originally planned to place the Freefall in one of the ride buildings where the Frog Hopper was located and even had it custom designed to fit in the space. When it arrived, however, the park realized that the heavier ride could place undue stress on that section of floor since there is a basement underneath. As a result, it was moved to its outside location.

Funland's biggest rides anchor the outdoor portion of the park.

Funland Today

Funland has become an institution along the boardwalk of this seaside community. It makes its presence known with a large two-story building that encloses much of the facility, but is open to the air and sunshine via large doors. Today, Funland features nineteen rides along with a wide array of midway and arcade games. The main entrance is off the boardwalk near Delaware Avenue and leads directly to the merry-go-round. Nearby are most of the kiddie rides including the classic fire engine, boats, and the Sky Fighter, which have all been around since the Sports Center days. The outdoor portion of the park is in the middle of the building and is home to the largest rides including the Chaos, the Sea Dragon, the Paratooper, and the Freefall. This area is also home to the helicopter ride that inspired the Fasnacht family to purchase the park. Beyond the outdoor area is another enclosed section that features the Gravitron, the Crazy Dazy, the Haunted Mansion, and bumper car rides.

Frontier Town Western Theme Park

OPENED 1959

ALTHOUGH ONLY SEPARATED BY A FEW MILES, FRONTIER TOWN IS TRULY a world apart from Ocean City's action-packed boardwalk. With its dusty streets, simple buildings, Indian village, and rodeo it would seem more at home in the American West rather than the marshlands along the Atlantic coast. It can be a welcome diversion in this community, however, and is a great example of the staple of the American family vacation in the 1950s and 1960s, the themed roadside attraction.

The Wild West Comes East

In the late 1950s entrepreneurs William Patton and William Pacy saw the popularity of themed roadside attractions spreading throughout the country. These facilities sought to capture much of their business from the emerging automobile culture and tended to follow two basic themes—fairy tales or the Old West. The two entrepreneurs felt that the resort area of Ocean City, Maryland, would be the perfect location for a western-themed facility. Not only had the town been a longtime favorite for vacationers, but the 1952 completion of the Bay Bridge made access to the town from Baltimore and Washington much easier for road-tripping families resulting in record crowds for the community.

The pair acquired a parcel of land west of town and hired Baltimore display artist Howard Adler to design the facility. Adler was well-known for his work in designing department store displays

Frontier Town Western Theme Park
P.O. Box 691
Ocean City, MD 21843
410-641-0057
info@frontiertown.com
www.frontiertown.com

in Baltimore, but had also created the characters for Enchanted Forest, a successful storybook-themed roadside attraction near Baltimore that opened in 1955.

Adler designed a replica of an 1860s western town with features such as a church, a barber shop, a general store, saloons, a dentist office, a post office, a jail, and a bank, all clustered around a main street. The new facility immediately caught the attention of the tourist trade, and the developers had to fence off the construction site to keep trespassing sightseers from being hurt by construction traffic.

In the summer of 1959, Frontier Town opened to eager throngs. The main street served as the heart of the attraction and a stage of sorts where a full variety of Wild West shows such as bank robberies and gunfights were acted out. Other attractions included a stagecoach ride, a pony trail, horseback riding, a deer park, and an Indian Village.

Following a successful first season, the park added a train ride. Purchased from Crown Metal Products of Wyano, Pennsylvania, the new ride was a 24-inch-gauge steam strain, complete with a coal-fired boiler. To celebrate the opening of the ride, the governor of Maryland came to the park to drive in a commemorative golden spike.

The 1961 season was a major transformational year for the increasingly popular Frontier Town. Several new attractions were added including an upgraded stagecoach ride, a kiddie handcar ride, and a Conestoga wagon offering a Trip to Friendly Forest. Other offerings included a blacksmith, trick riding, a petting zoo, panning for gold, a free shave in the barber shop, an archery range, and a horseshoe pitch.

Stagecoach rides have been a part of Frontier Town since it opened in 1959.

VISITING

FRONTIER TOWN WESTERN THEME PARK

LOCATION

Frontier Town is located on State Route 611 (Stephen Decatur Highway), 3$^1/_2$ miles south of the intersection with U.S. Route 50. The park will be on the left.

OPERATING SCHEDULE

Frontier Town opens in mid-June and operates through Labor Day. Hours are 10 A.M. to 6 P.M., although the gate closes at 4:30 P.M.

ADMISSION

Admission is around $15 and includes all rides, shows, and attractions with the exception of a nominal fee for horseback rides, panning for gold, and games in the Indian Village.

FOOD

The park features three food outlets. The largest is the Gold Nugget Saloon, which serves burgers, hot dogs, subs, chili, salads, and french fries. Shorty's Place offers breakfast items, barbecue, hot dogs, chili, popcorn, soda, and slushies. Also along the street is an ice cream parlor and candy store.

FOR CHILDREN

Frontier Town is a great family-oriented activity with all of the rides and shows being family friendly. Even the bandits on the stagecoach and train are fun.

SPECIAL FEATURES

Frontier Town is one of last remaining examples of the 1950s themed roadside attractions. It is a throwback to the 1950s as well as the 1860s.

Don't miss the Indian Village with its authentic dance shows and teepees. It is staffed by Native Americans who are happy to answer questions and share their culture.

TIME REQUIRED

Frontier Town, with its extensive lineup of live shows and numerous attractions can take up to six hours to completely experience. If you are pressed for time, three to four hours will give you a good overview of the offerings.

TOURING TIPS

Frontier Town western theme park is located adjacent to Frontier Town Water-park and Cowboy Golf. Combining the three is a great way to spend the day. Visit the water park in the morning and head on over to the western theme park for the afternoon. Note that the theme park, water park, and miniature golf all have separate admissions, but a combination ticket is available for the attractions.

The key additions that year, however, were the arrival of two families as part of efforts by Patton and Pacy to create as authentic a western experience as possible. Nelson Kennedy, an experienced rodeo cowboy, arrived from Frontier Town in North Hudson, New York, a similar facility opened by another group in 1952. "They stole my name, now they stole my help," his son Todd Kennedy recalls the owner of the New York park as saying.

In addition to operating a saddle shop along the main street, Kennedy put on a rodeo at the park for the first time, attracting 4,000 people on the first day alone.

Also coming to the park that season was John Moore, or Red Bird. A Cherokee Indian who acted in movies with Tonto and the Lone Ranger, he came to the park to set up a new Indian Village at the former location of the deer park. The village included displays of Indian culture and authentic dances. Red Bird's family, including his two children Aimee (Screaming Eagle) and John (Laughing Wolf), spent their summers at Frontier Town until 2006, when the Big Mountain family took over.

Spring storms in 1962 caused flooding that severely damaged the park, but Frontier Town was able to quickly bounce back, attracting 100,000 people. The new attraction that year was a riverboat ride, purchased from Adventure Town, a similar roadside attraction in Alexandria Bay, New York, that had recently shut down. In 1964, the Old Mine, a walk-through optical illusion attraction, opened in the woods near the Indian Village.

Frontier Town has one of the few steam-powered trains found in a theme park. It was added in 1960.

The riverboat was a featured attraction from 1962 to 1985.

Trying to Adapt to Changing Times

By the mid-1960s Frontier Town had peaked. With changing tastes and the declining popularity of westerns, the park found it an increasing challenge to remain relevant. Although a campground was opened next to the theme park in 1963, the rodeo was discontinued in 1965. The facility was acquired by the Parker family in 1969.

By 1981, however, business had fallen to half of the levels recorded in the early 1960s and the Parkers considered closing the theme park to concentrate on the campground. Fortunately Walter Hunter, a local restaurant owner, leased the facility and worked to turn it around. He brought back the rodeo in 1984 and replaced the aging riverboat with a paddleboat ride in 1986.

In 1996, the lease was acquired by Billy Waterman, who had worked at the park for twenty years. He again worked to upgrade the operation, traveling out west to look for ideas to ensure the attractions were authentic as possible. Unfortunately the rodeo again ended in 1997.

By 2005, however, Frontier Town was again struggling and its future was up in the air. Fortunately, Nelson Kennedy and his family, who had continued to spend their summers at the park, could not bear to see this disappearing piece of Americana fade away. They took over the lease and launched an upgrade of the park.

New historical displays such as the Chinese laundry, a bathhouse, and a schoolhouse were installed; existing facilities were upgraded; and the rodeo was brought back. Acquired also was the pony carousel, a horse-powered merry-go-round from Frontier Town in North Hudson, New York, which had closed in 1999.

The basic layout of Frontier Town has changed little from this early aerial view.

Frontier Town Western Theme Park Today

Frontier Town is a true survivor. One of dozens of themed attractions that opened along America's roadsides in the 1950s and 1960s, it is now one of the last of its kind. The park retains much of the charm it had in 1959 with its frontier-themed buildings clustered around a main street. Other attractions include a half-dozen rides, almost a dozen live shows daily, the Indian Village, and the Old Mine walk-through. Visitors enter through the frontier fort blockhouse, which opens onto the street. Here visitors find a variety of historical displays including a church, a barber shop, a dentist, a jail, a Chinese laundry, an undertaker, and a bank. The street is also the venue for many of the live shows that take place every day. These include the flag raising, a bank holdup, the Trial of Lopez, Billy Wilks Outlaw, and the Gunfight at the OK Corral. The Golden Nugget Saloon at the end of the street hosts the Can-Can Show twice a day.

The Rodeo arena is located behind the chapel. Behind the main street to the left are the rides including the stagecoach, the train, paddleboats, the pony carousel, horses, and the pony trail. Be on the lookout for bandits when you're on the stagecoach and train! Other attractions in this area include the schoolhouse, panning for gold, and the Old Mine. Don't miss the Indian Village with its authentic displays and Native American dancing shows.

Jolly Roger Amusement Park, Splash Mountain Water Park, Speedworld

OPENED 1965

FOR OVER FOUR DECADES A SMILING 40-FOOT-TALL PIRATE HAS SERVED as a landmark along this busy tourist strip in Ocean City, Maryland. Although he has remained steadfast, the land he oversees has changed dramatically. From a simple golf attraction, to a small amusement park, to a larger one, Jolly Roger Park has grown to the point that all of its features cannot be contained in one name. It now needs three—the Jolly Roger Amusement Park, the Splash Mountain water park, and the Speedworld go-cart complex.

Easing into It

Back in the early 1960s, Charles Jenkins, a local businessman who got his start with a cannery operation, acquired a large parcel of land that had just been created by filling in a portion of Assawoman Bay.

Through his company, Bay Shore Development, Jenkins built up much of the acreage, but retained 36 acres fronting Philadelphia Avenue, the town's main north-south artery. Given the high visibility of the parcel, Jenkins knew it needed to be put to use to take advantage of the growing tourist market in the seaside community. At the time, golf legend Arnold Palmer was constructing driving ranges and miniature golf courses around the country and came to Ocean City. Jenkins purchased a franchise and in July 1964 opened the Arnold Palmer Putting Course and Driving Range. By the time the season closed in mid-September,

Jolly Roger Amusement Park

2901 Coastal Highway
Ocean City, MD 21842

410-289-3477

info@jollyrogerpark.com
www.jollyrogerpark.com

the new operation had attracted 80,000 customers. Jenkins knew he was on to something.

For the next season, he decided to round out his offerings by adding a ten-ride amusement park. To oversee the construction, Jenkins hired Budco Associates, which had opened 110 Adventureland in East Farmingdale, New York, in 1962. Budco helped Jenkins create a sophisticated operation for its time with uniformed employees, corporate logos, and a well-balanced ride lineup.

Featured in that inaugural season were six rides from the Allan Herschell Company. Included were a merry-go-round, a Twister spinning ride, helicopters, a kiddie roller coaster, kiddie antique autos, and a train that still circles the park grounds. There were also three kiddie rides from Hampton Amusement Company, well-known for the distinctive colorful umbrella canopies on the top of each ride. Rounding out the lineup were a bumper car ride and the park's premier attraction, the Skyliner, a 700-foot-long sky ride. To compensate for the sandy soil, all of the rides were supported by 30-foot foundation pilings driven into the earth. The bumper cars alone had thirty of them to support their building. With the guidance of Budco, the $250,000 park was able to open a week ahead of schedule on Saturday, June 12, 1965.

Jolly Roger Amusement Park quickly established itself as a key tourist attraction in the community. Over the next decade it slowly grew and by

Jolly Roger originally opened with a focus on kiddie rides. It also featured a driving range, seen on the left.

LOCATION

Jolly Roger Amusement Park, Splash Mountain, and Speedworld are located on Philadelphia Avenue (aka Coastal Highway) at 30th Street. From U.S. Route 50, cross the H. Kelly Memorial Bridge over Sinepuxent Bay. Turn left on Baltimore Avenue to 30th Street. Turn left at 30th Street and the park will be in front of you. Free parking is available at the park.

OPERATING SCHEDULE

Jolly Roger Amusement Park is open Memorial Day weekend through Labor Day from 2 P.M. to midnight every day.

Splash Mountain water park is open Memorial Day weekend through Labor Day from 10 A.M. to 8 P.M. every day.

Speedworld is open Memorial Day weekend through Labor Day from 2 P.M. to midnight every day and weekends in April, May, September, and October from noon to 6 P.M.

ADMISSION

Admission to the Jolly Roger Amusement Park is free with a choice of paying by the ride or purchasing a one-price wristband. Visitors can obtain points on a Jolly Roger Passport to Fun card for approximately 60 cents each with rides taking between four and a half and eight points. Points are also good for the games.

The pay-one-price wristband costs under $20 and permits visitors to enjoy all rides and attractions.

Points and wristbands purchased at Jolly Roger Amusement Park can also be used at Jolly Roger at the Pier on the boardwalk.

Admission to Speedworld is also free with attractions being available on a pay-as-you-go basis, or you can purchase a pass for under $40 that gets you access to all tracks for two hours.

Access to Splash Mountain is via a one-price admission of under $35. Discounts are available for children under 42 inches tall and seniors.

Multipark admission plans are also available.

FOOD

There are six food stands located at Jolly Roger Amusement Park. The largest stand is near the front gate and kiddieland and features hot dogs, hamburgers, and other sandwiches. Splash Mountain also has one food stand.

FOR CHILDREN

Jolly Roger Amusement Park has approximately one dozen kiddie rides, most located at the front of the park, along with a fun house just for kids. In addition, the park features a number of family rides including the Wacky Worm roller coaster, a train, and a log flume.

Splash Mountain features three activity pools, while Speedworld has two kiddie tracks and a family track. (continued on page 94)

VISITING (continued from page 93)

JOLLY ROGER AMUSEMENT PARK, SPLASH MOUNTAIN WATER PARK, SPEEDWORLD

SPECIAL FEATURES

Splash Mountain is one of the largest water parks on the East Coast. There is something for almost everyone from quiet pools to high-speed slides.

With ten tracks, Speedworld has one of the most diverse lineups of go-carts in the country. If you are a go-carting enthusiast, it's a must-see.

TIME REQUIRED

It can easily occupy an entire day to fully experience Jolly Roger Amusement Park, Splash Mountain, and Speedworld. If your time is limited, the amusement park and Speedworld can be experienced in less than two hours each, although the water park would take more time.

TOURING TIPS

To avoid crowds, visit the amusement park and Speedworld during the afternoon, particularly on weekdays. Splash Mountain also tends to be less crowded on weekdays.

Don't fight for a parking space in the front of the park. Ample parking is usually available in the back parking lot behind the amusement park. This also gives you access to the less crowded rear entrance to Splash Mountain and to the rear bathhouse.

Admission plans purchased at Jolly Roger Amusement Park can also be used at Jolly Roger at the Pier on the boardwalk. So if you plan to visit both, plan accordingly to get the most for your money.

1975 featured eight major and fourteen kiddie rides, twice the number as when the park opened. Included was the park's first major roller coaster, a compact steel model from Italy named Gallassia.

Rounding Out the Fun

In 1976, Jolly Roger sought to expand its appeal to a wider variety of visitors by adding two go-cart tracks including the Formula 1, which featured miniature race cars on a winding course, along with a stadium featuring a dolphin show.

The next major addition came in 1983, when Jolly Roger Park acquired a 591-foot-long log flume. Originally built in 1980 for Beech Bend Amusement Park, Bowling Green, Kentucky, by Arrow Development, it also operated at the 1982 World's Fair in Knoxville, Tennessee, before coming to its new home. The log flume foreshadowed a transformational event that occurred a couple of years later when the first phases of the Splash Mountain water park were constructed.

Although the park was placing an increasing emphasis on go-carts, shows, and water attractions, the traditional amusements were not for-

The Looping Star roller coaster (left) and log flume were two major attractions that were added in the 1980s.

gotten. In 1984, the Looping Star, a large steel roller coaster built by legendary roller coaster designer Anton Schwarzkopf, made a two-year appearance at the park. Standing 61 feet tall, the ride featured a twisting first drop and a vertical loop along its 1,800-foot-long course. The Looping Star was the largest of several amusement park rides added during this period including the Flying Swings, the Spider, the Mirror Maze, the Himalaya, and a walk-through Haunted House.

By the mid-1980s, the Jolly Roger Amusement Park was in a major growth mode offering a wide array of attractions. These included a full-scale amusement park; several live shows; a petting zoo; the Splash Mountain water park; and Speedworld, a new area developed around

Splash Mountain water park was developed in the mid-1980s.

King Kobra was one of the major roller coasters that appeared at the park in the late 1980s. It was sold in 1989. ERIC SAKOWSKI

the Formula 1 race track. Speedworld also featured Bumper Boats; Skeeter Boats, miniature speed boats in a large pond; and additional go-cart tracks.

The removal of the Looping Star in 1985 left Jolly Roger without a major roller coaster, a situation that was resolved in 1987 when two major roller coasters were acquired. The first, the Time Twister, was a 75-foot-tall, 2,400-foot-long looping roller coaster built by Vekoma of the Netherlands. It was acquired from Traumland Park, Bottrop, Germany, and featured two corkscrew inversions.

Nearby, the King Kobra was erected. Standing 138 feet tall, it became the tallest structure in the park. King Kobra originally opened in 1977 at Kings Dominion, Doswell, Virginia, as the first shuttle loop coaster designed by Anton Schwarzkopf. The shuttle loop is a unique style of roller coaster in which the train is catapulted out of the station by dropping a 40-ton weight in a tower at the end of the ride. Connected to a launch system in the track, the train accelerates to a top speed of 53 miles per hour in a matter of seconds, the riders travel through a vertical loop and up a 70-degree incline until the train's momentum is depleted. It then falls backward, again traveling through the loop.

Although the 1987 season was the first for the new roller coasters, the Skyliner gave its final rides.

As the 1980s ended, the King Kobra was sold to Alton Towers, Staffordshire, United Kingdom, to make room for additional parking, and the dolphin show entertained its final visitors.

Creating a Balance

The 1990s were a decade of transition for the complex. As it began, the increasingly popular Speedworld underwent a major expansion. Three tracks were added in 1990, followed by one each in 1993 and 1994 as it grew to its eventual assortment of ten different tracks ranging from the Kiddie Track to the Grand Prix and Formula 1.

Meanwhile, growth continued in Splash Mountain. The pond where the Skeeter Boats and Bumper Boats operated was filled in to create more room for new water attractions. Joining the original Body and Double Tube slide were a kiddie water area in 1991, a 1,000-foot-long lazy river in 1995, and 5 waterslides relocated from Ocean City Pier in 1996—the Black Hole and Cannonball, each with two slides, and the single chute Tower Tube. By 1998, the water park was so successful that management doubled its size with the expansion of the Lazy River and the addition of the Lost Lagoon water play area.

Since its opening in 1990, Speedworld has grown into one of the largest go-kart facilities in the country.

With the popularity of the expanded Splash Mountain and Speedworld, it became necessary to consolidate the amusement park at the now space-constrained facility to create additional room for parking. The Time Twister was sold to Genting Theme Park in Malaysia in 1993, and other rides such as the Paratrooper and the Haunted House were removed as well as a petting zoo and the live shows. Meanwhile other rides such as the log flume and the Bumper Cars were moved to new locations in the park.

Although the amusement park was restructured in the 1990s, that did not mean new rides were not appearing. Throughout much of the later part of the decade, Jolly Roger would keep the park fresh by bringing in roller coasters for brief appearances before moving them to other locations. A Mad Mouse appeared in 1996, followed by the Firecracker, a compact twisting roller coaster operated for a single season in 1998. It originally entertained visitors at Holiday World, Santa Claus, Indiana, for sixteen years. Then came the Wildcat, which operated from 1999 to 2001. Built by Anton Schwarzkopf, it stood 50 feet high and featured 1,800 feet of track. It was obtained from Valleyfair!, Shakopee, Minnesota.

But roller coasters were not the only rides opening at Jolly Roger Amusement Park during this period. In 1996, the original merry-go-round was replaced by a double-decker merry-go-round imported from Italy, and 1998 saw four kiddie rides including the Helicopters and the

The Wacky Worm and Wild Mouse roller coasters were installed in 2004. The Wild Mouse was replaced in 2007.

Speedway, added along with the Nightmare Manor dark ride. The Sky-coaster replaced the Bumper Boats and it thrilled riders with its giant free-falling swing until 2006.

New rides continued to be added in the twenty-first century, including the Giant Wheel, which opened for a two-season run in 2000 after being acquired from Kennywood, West Mifflin, Pennsylvania, and two new roller coasters were erected in 2002. For smaller visitors, the Wacky Worm provided a gentle figure-eight-shaped ride standing 13 feet high with 450 feet of track. Thrill seekers could enjoy the Wild Mouse. Built by the German firm of Maurer Söhne, the ride was an updated version of the old style mouse that relied on hairpin turns rather than sharp drops for thrills. Standing nearly 50 feet tall, it had 1,200 feet of track.

Ever since it opened, Splash Mountain has become increasingly popular. As a result recent years have been highlighted by constant expansion, making it one of the largest water parks in the middle Atlantic region. In 2000, Stealth a large U-shaped slide was installed, followed in 2001 by the 500-foot-long Master Blaster. This unique waterslide is best described as a water coaster as it uses water jets to propel riders up and down hills on the slide. Master Blaster was followed by the Wave Pool in 2002, the Rainforest in 2003, a six-lane racing slide in 2005, and in 2007 the Eye of the Hurricane bowl slide where riders plunge into a large bowl and travel around it before falling through the middle. Meanwhile, the Wild Mouse was replaced by the Racing Coaster, a twisting steel track roller coaster standing 25 feet tall with 1,200 feet of track.

Jolly Roger Amusement Park, Splash Mountain, and Speedworld Today

From its humble beginnings as a miniature golf course and driving range, Jolly Roger Amusement Park has evolved into a multifaceted, integrated entertainment complex consisting of an amusement park, a water park, a go-cart park, and two miniature golf courses. The amusement park is home to approximately thirty rides and attractions including two roller coasters, a dark ride, a log flume, and a mirror maze. Splash Mountain features nearly twenty different water attractions ranging from pools to splash around in to high-speed water slides for thrill seekers. Speedworld is home to one of the largest collections of go-cart tracks anywhere.

The facility faces Philadelphia Avenue where the main entrance to the amusement park is located. At the front of the park are most of the kiddie rides, along with the Jungle Golf miniature golf course. Behind the kiddieland are the park's larger rides arranged roughly in a circle. Going left, one passes the train station, the mirror maze, the Nightmare Manor

Splash Mountain has grown into one of the largest water parks in the region.

dark ride, the log flume, and the Racing Coaster and Wacky Worm roller coasters. A rear entrance to the amusement park is also in this area as are the bumper car ride and the midway games. Splash Mountain and Speedworld share a common entrance on the north side of the property, just past the Treasure Hunt miniature golf course, although a second entrance to both facilities is located in the back of the facility, near the rear entrance to the amusement park.

Funland
Family Fun Center

OPENED 1971

TOM KUHN WAS A PHYSICAL EDUCATION TEACHER LOOKING FOR SOMETHING to do to occupy his summers. Naturally he was drawn to a seasonal business that he could shut down once vacationers went back for the start of school in the fall. His journey culminated in the opening of Funland.

A Road Runs through It

In the 1960s, the resort community surrounding Deep Creek Lake in western Maryland was a cool, quiet mountain getaway. "It was just a little town with Pittsburgh steelworkers building summer homes," Kuhn said but that would soon change as improvements to the regional road system started attracting vacationers from a wider area.

One of those roads was the new U.S. Route 219, a modern highway that provided improved north-south access. A side effect of the construction was that several 10- to 20-acre "farmlets" at the north end of the lake were split in half.

One of those split parcels was a 4-acre site in the village of McHenry. At the gateway to the resort area, it fronted on the busy new highway; and there were no other nearby entertainment venues to cater to the tourist trade. It was the perfect place for Kuhn to realize his dreams.

He went to work on upgrading the site and in the summer of 1971 opened Funland. It was a

**Funland
Family Fun Center**
24450 Garrett Highway
(U.S. Route 219)
McHenry, MD 21541

301-387-6168

www.deepcreeklake
.com/funland

simple operation consisting of an open-air arcade building, which had no heating or air conditioning, and a go-cart track featuring a roadway composed of tar and stone chips with guardrails made out of hay bales.

The new operation met an unfilled need, and in 1972 Kuhn expanded the fledgling operation with the addition of a miniature golf course. On his way, he had a vision of continuing his expansion by adding a merry-go-round and a Ferris wheel. Unfortunately, zoning problems and the lack of a modern sewer system temporarily put his plans on hold.

Growing Up

For the next several years Kuhn worked to resolve the issues so that he could again begin growing his operation. Unfortunately in the interim, rising insurance costs forced the closure of the original go-cart track. It was replaced by a new go-cart track with modern cars and safety features in the early 1990s. In 1994, the final issues related to Funland's zoning were resolved and the sewer system installed. Now Kuhn could get down to business.

Funland was totally transformed for the 1994 season. The old plywood arcade building was demolished, and a substantial new arcade and food service building was erected in its place. A Super Collider bumper car ride was installed next to the go-carts, and Kuhn's long desired merry-go-round was finally realized.

Kuhn found the ride in a classified advertisement in *Amusement Business,* an industry trade magazine. It is something of a piece of history.

Funland features a wooden merry-go-round among its attractions.

LOCATION

Funland Family Fun Center is located in McHenry, Maryland, on U.S. Route 219, approximately 13 miles south of Exit 14A off Interstate 68.

OPERATING SCHEDULE

Starting on Easter weekend, Funland is open at noon on Friday, Saturday, and Sunday. Between Memorial Day weekend and Labor Day, the park is open at 10 A.M. daily. Weekend operation then resumes from September through Thanksgiving. Closing time varies depending on the crowd in the park.

ADMISSION

Admission to Funland is free with attractions available on a pay-as-you-go basis. The cost ranges from around $2 for the merry-go-round to $6 for the miniature golf course.

FOOD

The pizza shop in the arcade building features pizza, submarine sandwiches, and ice cream.

FOR CHILDREN

The merry-go-round is a timeless favorite of children. In addition, children six and under can enjoy miniature golf at a discount price, and kids as young as four can ride along with an adult in the go-carts.

SPECIAL FEATURES

The merry-go-round was manufactured during a transitional time in the development of the ride. Although the body of each horse is made of wood, the heads, legs, and tails are all cast aluminum.

TIME REQUIRED

Two hours should be sufficient to fully experience Funland including a round on the miniature golf course.

TOURING TIPS

Visit in the afternoon to avoid the largest crowds.

Manufactured in 1951 or 1952 by the Allan Herschell Company, it was built at a transitional time among merry-go-round manufacturers in which wooden horses were giving way to horses made of aluminum and fiberglass. As a result, the horses on Funland's machine feature wooden bodies, but the head, legs, and tails are cast aluminum.

With the 1994 expansion, Kuhn's original dreams had come to fruition, but improvements continued. A climbing wall was installed in 2001. By 2003 the original miniature golf course had become dated and was no longer challenging to an increasingly sophisticated audience, so Funland replaced it with an elaborate new course featuring a waterfall, a cave, and a stream.

Funland Today

From a simple summer job, Funland has grown into a full-time business featuring a large arcade, a miniature golf course, a go-cart track, bumper cars, a merry-go-round, a climbing wall, and a water wars game. The arcade building serves as the main entrance. The miniature golf course is located off to one side, and the remaining attractions are located behind the building.

Kings Dominion

OPENED 1974

A MINIATURE VERSION OF THE FAMED EIFFEL TOWER IS PROBABLY ONE OF the last things a person would expect to see along this busy stretch of Interstate 95 north of Richmond, Virginia. For over 30 years, however, it has served as a beacon to travelers that Kings Dominion is waiting to entertain them.

Distinguished Roots

Kings Dominion has unique roots in the business, stretching far beyond its 1974 opening to 1924 when George Schott took over Coney Island in Cincinnati, Ohio. Over the next several decades, his family built the park into what was generally regarded as one of the best-run amusement parks in the country. Walt Disney even visited the facility in the 1950s looking for ideas on how to run a quality operation when he was building Disneyland. By the 1960s, however, Coney Island was becoming a victim of its own success. Crowds were increasing, expansion room was limited, and flooding from the adjacent Ohio River was a constant nuisance. As a result, the park merged with Taft Broadcasting in 1969 and started making plans to relocate to a new site north of Cincinnati. There would be plenty of room for growth, providing Coney Island the opportunity to transform itself into a major regional theme park. In 1972, Kings Island opened, continuing many of the traditions that made Coney Island such an institution, such as wooden roller coasters and a large kiddieland. Kings Island was an immediate success and Taft Entertainment, Taft Broadcasting's

Kings Dominion
P.O. Box 2000
Doswell, VA 23047
(804) 876-5000
www.kingsdominion.com

theme park division, started looking for the next location for one of its theme parks.

The busy corridor along Interstate 95 in Virginia soon emerged as a top candidate. The highway was a key route from the densely populated northeastern states to Florida. It provided easy access to markets such at Washington, D.C., and Richmond, and at the time, there was no other theme park in the region. A 1,300-acre site was purchased, and in April 1973 construction started on the $60 million development. It was the second most expensive theme park project up to that time, trailing only the Magic Kingdom at Walt Disney World.

To complement the theme park, Taft teamed up with Lion Country Safari, Incorporated, which had built successful drive-through animal parks in California, Florida, and Texas, to develop an animal attraction. The thought was to open the safari attraction ahead of the rest of the park using its established brand to draw people to a preview center to promote Kings Dominion. By April 1974, construction had progressed to the point where the preview center was ready for visitors.

The heart of the preview center was what would eventually be the Lion Country Safari area of the completed park. The main feature was a $5 million, 80-acre drive-through safari where visitors could enjoy dozens of African animals in natural settings along a two-mile-long road. Also included was a thirty-minute movie showing the completed park and the Scooby Doo, a small wooden roller coaster that would eventually anchor the new park's kiddie area. Built by the Philadelphia Toboggan Company, one of the most prolific roller coaster builders in history, the coaster was perfect for beginning riders and their families, standing 35 feet tall with a top speed of 35 miles per hour along its 1,385 feet of track.

It was obvious that the public was looking forward to the debut of Kings Dominion as by the time the season ended, 650,000 people had visited the preview center.

Throughout the fall and winter, workers scrambled to complete construction on the remainder of the facility. Like its sister park in Ohio, Kings Dominion borrowed heavily on European culture for its design. Not only was the park adorned with outdoor restaurants, flowers, flags, and fountains, but the focal point of the park was the replica of France's Eiffel Tower.

Standing 330 feet tall, the tower is a one-third scale replica of the Paris original and was designed by Intamin AG of Switzerland, a leading manufacturer of theme park attractions. Intamin fabricated the 700-ton attraction in Europe and shipped it to the site in pieces where it was erected atop 16-foot foundations. Today, it offers elevator rides to the 280- and 300-foot levels providing a spectacular view of the park and

LOCATION

Kings Dominion is located just off Exit 98 of Interstate 95, approximately 20 miles north of Richmond and 75 miles south of Washington, D.C.

OPERATING SCHEDULE

Kings Dominion is open weekends in April and May, daily from Memorial Day weekend through Labor Day, and most weekends in September and October. The park is closed for private events on some weekends in September, so check before visiting. Kings Dominion opens at 10:30 A.M. with closing time varying from 6 to 10 P.M., depending on the time of year.

ADMISSION

A pay-one-price admission of around $45 entitles visitors to all rides and attractions with the exception of games and attractions such as the Xtreme SkyFlyer and the go-carts. Two-day tickets are also available along with discounted passes for those under 48 inches tall or sixty-two or more years of age. Guests can also visit in the evening at a reduced rate. Parking is an extra fee. Discounted tickets can be purchased via the Internet on the park's website.

FOOD

Kings Dominion offers over fifty food service facilities ranging from portable carts to full-service restaurants. Major outlets include Country Kitchen in Old Virginia for ribs and chicken; Happy Days Diner in The Grove serving burgers, chicken, and fries; Victoria Pizza also in The Grove featuring pizza and pasta; Bubba Gump's Shrimp Shack for seafood; and Congo Grill and Pizza for hot dogs and pizza. Several franchised outlets are located throughout the park including Subway, Chik-Fil-A, and Boardwalk Fries.

FOR CHILDREN

KidZville is the main children's area offering ten kiddie rides, two roller coasters, and a large play area. Next door, Nickelodeon Central is home to the Rugrats Toontike, where kids can drive their own cars, and the Green Slime Zone, a damp play area. It is also the best place to meet all of your favorite Nickelodeon characters.

The park also has a number of other rides and attractions that can be enjoyed by most members of the family including the Avalanche roller coaster, the Flying Eagles, the Shenandoah Lumber Company log flume, and the Scooby Doo and the Haunted Mansion dark ride.

WaterWorks offers two play areas—Surf City Splash House and Lil' Barefoot Beach for the smaller visitors. Lazy Rider and the wave pools are also a great place for the family to splash around.

(continued on page 108)

VISITING (continued from page 107)

KINGS DOMINION

SPECIAL FEATURES

Kings Dominion has one of the largest and most diverse collections of roller coasters anywhere. Included in its lineup are four wooden roller coasters—the most of any amusement park in the country—including the Rebel Yell, a twin-track racing coaster; the Grizzly, a re-creation of a 1920s' classic; Hurler, with its banked curves and airtime hills; and Scooby Doo's Ghoster Coaster, a great starter ride. Steel coaster aficionados can enjoy Shockwave, one of the first stand-up roller coasters; the multiloop Anaconda and Dominator; and the Ricochet, a throwback to a 1950s' wild mouse. Kings Dominion also has the largest collection of launched roller coasters in the world. Volcano, The Blast Coaster is the most intense with two launch sections, one of which sends the train straight up through the top of a mountain. Others include the indoor Flight of Fear and the themed The Italian Job Turbo Coaster. Don't miss Avalanche, a bobsled roller coaster that is the only ride of its kind in North America.

The 305-foot Drop Zone is one of the tallest tower rides in the world and its 272-foot drop is one of the most thrilling experiences in any theme park.

The Eiffel Tower is the heart of the park and provides a spectacular view of Kings Dominion and the surrounding countryside from thirty stories in the air.

Don't miss Kings Dominion's classic carousel. Hand-carved in 1917, it is one of the finest examples of this American art form.

TIME REQUIRED

Plan to spend at least one full day at Kings Dominion, with a second day being optimal. If you are pressed for time and visit on a day when crowds are light, the major attractions can be enjoyed in about six hours.

TOURING TIPS

Purchase your ticket online ahead of time on the park's website. Not only will you be able to avoid lines at the front gate, but Kings Dominion offers special online-only discounts.

Try to visit Kings Dominion on a weekday, particularly early in the season when the park tends to be less crowded. Sundays in the fall also tend to have lighter crowds.

Arrive just before the park opens and try to hit the Congo-themed area first to get in its four roller coasters before the crowd reaches that area.

Don't forget that there are two sections to the WaterWorks water park. Crowds tend to reach the wooded section on the far side of the Rebel Yell last. Also remember that there are two changing areas. The one on the far side of the Rebel Yell is usually less crowded.

Kings Dominion has several height-check stations in the park. Have your kids measured and they will receive a color-coded wristband.

Kings Dominion's Eiffel Tower has served as the heart of the park since 1975. It is one-third the size of the Paris original.
KINGS DOMINION

surrounding countryside. The total cost for the tower was $2.2 million, about $500,000 more than it cost to build the Paris original in 1887.

By May 3, 1975, Kings Dominion was ready for visitors. Sprawling over 200 acres were five themed areas with more than twenty rides and dozens of other attractions. The park entrance opened up onto International Street, one of the most dramatic entrances in the industry. Arranged around a 320-foot-long, $1 million programmed fountain were four European-style buildings that featured a variety of shops and restaurants. At the end of the street was the Eiffel Tower.

Beyond the tower was Old Virginia, which drew upon the history of the state in its building styles and theming. The main attraction was the Shenandoah Lumber Company, a 1,500-foot-long log flume from Arrow Dynamics, the inventor of the theme park staple. Other attractions included the Blue Ridge Tollway, an antique auto ride; the Old Dominion railroad, featuring two ten-ton steam locomotives; and the 1,300-seat Mason-Dixon Music Hall.

Candy Apple Grove was next. Themed after an old-fashioned amusement park, the area was dominated by the Rebel Yell, a $1.5 million twin track wooden roller coaster. Built by the Philadelphia Toboggan Company, the ride stands 92 feet tall and features 3,368 feet of track on each side. The Rebel Yell traveled alongside Lake Charles, a 10-acre lake named after project manager Charles Flatt, that featured a $500,000 fountain shooting water 250 feet in sky, twice the height of Old Faithful. Unfortunately as Dennis Spiegel, the park's first general manager soon realized, when the fountain was turned on to full power, "it watered everyone in the park!"

Joining the Rebel Yell in Candy Apple Grove was a second roller coaster, the Galaxie, a smaller steel track model from Italy that featured a combination of drops and tight turns along 1,650 feet of track. But

Candy Apple Grove was the largest section at King's Dominion when it opened.
KINGS DOMINION

Candy Apple Grove featured more than roller coasters. Other attractions included a sky ride, a Wave Swinger swing ride, flying skooters, bumper cars, and other rides.

The area was also home to Kings Dominion's antique carousel. A true work of art, the ride was originally carved by the Philadelphia Toboggan Company in 1917 and features sixty-six horses arranged in four rows. The carousel originally operated at Riverside Park in Springfield, Massachusetts, until the park closed in 1938 as a result of the Depression. It was then moved to Roger Williams Park, Providence, Rhode Island, from whom Kings Dominion purchased it in 1973 for $100,000. Over the next sixteen months, it was painstakingly restored. Up to eighteen layers of paint were removed and it was discovered that about fifteen horses were held together only by their paint.

Hanna Barbera Land served as the kiddie area. It was anchored by the Scooby Doo coaster and also featured a turnpike car ride, four kiddie rides, the Treasure Cave walk-through, a dolphin show, and the other end of the sky ride.

Rounding out the themed areas was Lion Country Safari, which had served the park so well as the preview area. The safari was expanded to 120 acres and a $3 million, two-mile-long monorail was built to transport guests through three sections of African animals. There was also a bird show, a petting farm, and an animal nursery.

With such a well-rounded lineup of attractions, visitors flocked to the new facility and attendance topped 1.8 million its first season.

Growing Up

The success of the first season prompted Kings Dominion to launch a $2.5 million expansion for 1976 that featured four new rides including the Apple Turnover, which flips riders head over heels; Mount Kilimanjaro, a high-speed bobsled ride built into a 50-foot-high mountain; a Scrambler; and a kiddie Ferris wheel.

The following year, a new roller coaster debuted in Lion Country Safari along the shore of Lake Charles. King Kobra, built at a cost of nearly $1 million, represented a new genre of roller coaster known as the shuttle loop. Consisting of a long straight 720-foot-long stretch of track, riders are catapulted out of the station by dropping a 40-ton counterweight in a tower at the end of the ride. Connected to a launch system in the track, the train accelerates to a top speed of 53 miles per hour in a matter of seconds; the riders travel through a 46-foot-tall vertical loop and up a 70-degree 138-foot-tall incline until its momentum is depleted. It then falls backward, again traveling through the loop. King Kobra was the first shuttle loop coaster designed by Anton Schwarzkopf, the renowned designer of steel roller coasters who went on to sell a dozen similar models around the world.

The park also received national publicity that season when it was featured prominently in the movie *Roller Coaster.* The combination of the movie and King Kobra led to a record attendance of almost 2 million people for the season.

Expansion in 1978 was a little more modest with a new water skiing show in Lake Charles and six new kiddie rides in Hanna Barbera Land, but work was already underway on the park's next spectacular attraction. According to Spiegel, because of rising competition in the area, he felt the park needed some-

King Kobra was the first ride of its kind when it opened in 1978. It remained at the park until 1986. JIM ABBATE

The Lost World was a massive attraction that opened in 1979 containing three separate rides.

thing "unique, that had never been done before with such mass that people would be drawn to it."

The result was a 170-foot-tall mountain dubbed the Lost World. Opened in 1979 after two and a half years of planning and construction, the $7 million attraction contained three rides, including two dark rides. Voyage to Atlantis was a 1,432-foot-long flume ride that traveled through the mountain on a five-and-a-half minute journey to the lost continent, culminating in a plunge down a 50 foot hill. Land of Dooz took riders on a train ride to an underground world populated by Doozies, small creatures that make everything work on the surface of the earth. Also in the mountain was the Time Shaft, a special effects ride in which guests stand up in a large barrel. As the barrel spins, they are pinned against the wall and the floor drops. The Lost World was connected to the smaller 55-foot-tall mountain, which was home to the Mt. Kilimanjaro bobs, creating one large range.

Although the Lost World as a whole was well received, park officials thought the Voyage to Atlantis could be improved. In 1979, the park rethemed the ride as the Haunted River. The ambitious renovation included six rooms—the Piranha River, the Bermuda Triangle, the Nile River, the Black Lagoon, the Amazon River, and the Dismal Swamp—populated by sixty skeletons, twenty-five of which were animated, along with thirty other animated figures and even four live actors.

Kings Dominion again took a break from expanding in 1981, but preparations were well under way for their next spectacular attraction. In a heavily wooded corner of Old Virginia construction was under way on a wooden roller coaster. At the time, there were only a couple of individuals in the world who were capable of building such a ride. As a result, Taft Entertainment used its own staff to oversee construction, basing the ride on the Wildcat, a classic from the 1920s that thrilled riders at Coney Island, the park's ancestral home, from 1926 to 1964. Standing 87 feet tall, Grizzly's 3,150 feet of track snake through the woods, featuring twisting first drop and a tight figure-eight-shaped layout.

The dense woods of Old Virginia also served as the setting for Kings Dominion's next attraction. Ready for the 1983 season was White Water Canyon, a $3 million ride that provides a simulated trip down white-water rapids. Built by Intamin, of Switzerland, the ride features round six-passenger boats that travel down an 1,800-foot river surrounded by 30-ton boulders and 15-foot canyonlike walls. Four geysers spray water 20 feet in the air, and three waterfalls drench riders.

In 1984, the Doozies were evicted from the Lost World. Moving in were the Smurfs, the tiny blue creatures who transformed the Land of Dooz into Smurf Mountain, featuring six sections showing Smurfs at work and play. The $1.2 million improvement program also included the installation of Berserker, a $500,000 looping boat swing that flips riders in a series of 360 arcs.

Changing Hands

By now, Taft Broadcasting was seeking to focus its efforts on broadcasting and exit the theme park business. As a result, it sold Kings Dominion and its sister parks—Kings Island in Ohio, Carowinds in North Carolina, and Canada's Wonderland near Toronto—to company management in a $167 million leveraged buyout.

But the sale did not rob momentum from Kings Dominion. In 1985, Diamond Falls opened in the Congo, the renamed Lion Country Safari area. Diamond Falls was an updated version of one of the oldest types of amusement ride—the shoot-the-chutes. Dating back to 1889, the shoot-the-chutes was one of the first water rides, sending a boat down an incline into a splashdown pool. It became a staple at most larger parks in the early part of the twentieth century, but by the 1980s, it had largely disappeared. A modern version was created for the 1984 World's Fair in New Orleans and Kings Dominion was quick to order a version from Intamin for their park. It was the first modern shoot-the-chutes to be located in a theme park, taking riders up a 50-foot hill, around a turn, and down into the splashdown.

The new owners followed up in 1986, the last year of operation for King Kobra, with the addition of Shockwave. Replacing the Galaxie in Candy Apple Grove, Shockwave represented a new type of roller coaster that was taking the country by storm in which riders traveled in trains while standing up. On the $3 million Shockwave, the train climbs a 95-foot-tall hill, then plunges down an 84-foot drop and through a vertical loop and a 540-degree spiral banked a nearly 90 degrees along 2,231 feet of track. The sensation created by Shockwave brought record throngs to the park, with attendance passing 2 million for the first time.

New types of water rides were becoming staples in theme parks around the world during the 1980s. Kings Dominion had already enjoyed success during the decade with White Water Canyon and Diamond Falls. In 1987 they rounded out their water ride assortment with the addition of Racing Rivers. Replacing the turnpike, the $750,000 attraction included three different types of waterslides that guests could enjoy in their street clothes. The slides included Riptide, where guests ride on sleds down a 30-foot hill; Splashdown, on which riders travel down an undulating trough in rubber rafts; and Torpedo, an enclosed twisting tube slide.

Attention again switched back to roller coasters in 1988 with the debut of Avalanche. Located in the Congo, Avalanche is based on the Flying Turns rides of the 1930s on which trains traveled freely down a trough. Built by Heinrich Mack GMBH and Company, a German manufacturer that got its start manufacturing carriages in 1780, Avalanche stands 60 feet high with 1,900 feet of steel trough. It is the only ride of its kind in North America.

Although Kings Dominion's youngest visitors were enjoying a five-ride expansion of Hanna Barbera Land in 1990, thrill seekers were more

The Avalanche bobsled roller coaster remains the only ride of its type in North America. KINGS DOMINION

interested in the activity in Lake Charles. During the winter of 1990, the lake had been drained so that the park could begin construction on its next roller coaster. Once spring came, however, the park filled the lake back in and for the rest of the season, the half-completed structure teased guests about the thrills to come. Once the 1990 season ended, construction resumed; and soon the exact nature of the ride was known.

Dubbed Anaconda, the new $5 million roller coaster was built by Arrow Dynamics, then the world's leading manufacturer of steel roller coasters. Opened in spring 1991, the ride stands 128 feet tall and features a 144-foot drop into a tunnel under the waters of Lake Charles. The massive roller coaster arrived at the park in the form of twenty-one tractor trailer loads of support columns and twenty-two train cars of track. The 2,700-foot-long ride flips riders upside down four times over Lake Charles including a vertical loop, a double corkscrew, and the first double inversion Butterfly element. With a year to wait, thrill seekers were eager to get on the ride, and attendance set new records.

The Movies Come to Virginia

The opening of Anaconda was not the only major change Lake Charles saw in 1991. Toward the end of the year, the portion of the lake closest to Candy Apple Grove was filled in to create room for Hurricane Reef, a 7-acre water park. The $4.5 million development provided another major experience with five waterslide towers featuring fifteen different waterslides, along with a lazy river and kid's play area.

Although Hurricane Reef did give the park a new identity, another transformation occurred later in the year when Paramount Communications, Inc., the movie studio, reached an agreement to acquire Kings Entertainment and its five theme parks. Like several of their competitors, Paramount saw the theme park chain as an excellent platform to promote its movies and moved quickly to do so.

The 1993 season marked the final year for the Safari Monorail and related animal attractions, but the new owners erected the Action FX Theater. It is a simulator attraction with two theaters that each feature seventy-four seats synchronized to the action projected on 26-by-59-foot screens. For the first year, the attraction revolved around the movie *Days of Thunder*. It has since undergone several incarnations.

The theater was just the first of several attractions—themed to Paramount brands—to debut at the park. In 1994, guests could be transported to Wayne's World, a new 8-acre themed area featuring highlights of the popular movie including Stan Mikita's Restaurant, shops, and two rides—Screamweaver, a flying skooter ride relocated from elsewhere in the park, and Hurler, the "first movie themed wooden roller coaster in

Wayne's World was one of the movie themed additions installed during the Paramount era. DAVID HAHNER

North America." Designed and built by International Coasters, Inc., Hurler featured a unique 3,157-foot-long layout with an 80-foot drop that leads to a series of high speed curves, and low airtime hills. Hurler was Kings Dominion's fourth wooden roller coaster, giving it more than any park in the country.

Following the successful debut of Wayne's World, Paramount's Kings Dominion, as the park was then called, opened in 1995 the first location of a Nickelodeon-themed attraction outside Nickelodeon Studios in Florida. The 3-acre Nickelodeon Splat City is anchored by the Green Slime Zone, an interactive pipe work water maze, among other participatory activities.

By the mid-1990s, the industry was locked in the largest roller coaster arms race in history. Although the race for the tallest and fastest ride played a key role in this competition, many parks sought to stake their claim by introducing rides using groundbreaking technology. In 1996, Paramount's Kings Dominion made its entry with Flight of Fear. Rather than the traditional lift hill, this roller coaster relies on a first of its kind linear induction motor (LIM) launch system to launch the ride from 0 to 54 miles per hour in just four seconds before the 2,705-foot-long ride negotiates a 78-foot-high, 500-ton, twisted jumble of tracks that includes four inversions along with thirty vertical and twenty-five horizontal turns. To compound the thrill, the entire ride is enclosed in a 1-acre building and complemented with outer space theming.

As Jim Seay, president of ride manufacturer Premier Rides explains the technology, "An electric current shoots down the length of the launch creating a magnetic force. Aluminum fins attached to the side of the trains act as conductors and pass through the LIMs propelling the vehicle forward. The coaster train literally 'surfs' the magnetic wave down the track at rocket speeds, blasting up into the heart of the ride."

The park's younger visitors received the bulk of the attention in 1997 when Racing Rivers was removed as part of the conversion of Hanna Barbera Land into KidZville. The new area kept the best of the old including the Scooby Doo roller coaster, which was renamed the Ghoster Coaster, and added several new attractions. This included the Taxi Jam, an 8-foot-tall, 205-footlong kiddie coaster, and the Kidz Construction Company, a huge play area that included a real cement mixer and dump truck outfitted with play elements.

As had become tradition, while the park's guests were enjoying the park's newest attractions, work was already underway on the next big thing. In the Congo, construction was under way to outfit the Lost World rides with another roller coaster. Work had actually been going on for sometime with Smurf Mountain being retired in 1993 and the Haunted River and Time Shaft rides entertaining their last guests in 1994. By the end of the 1997 season, however, visitors could tell something unusual was happening. Given the mountain structure, it was easy for the ride's designers to come up with a theme—Volcano, The Blast Coaster was born.

Volcano, The Blast Coaster took up residence in the Lost World mountain in 1998.

Like Flight of Fear, Volcano, The Blast Coaster uses a series of linear induction motors to propel the trains. But for the first time on a LIM-powered roller coaster, trains were suspended underneath the track. The 2,757-foot-long ride, which was manufactured by the Swiss firm of Intamin AG, begins with the trains being launched, from 0 to 70 miles per hour in four seconds, out of the mountain and through a large turn. After returning to the mountain, a second set of motors boosts the train 155 feet straight up through the top in a fiery eruption. The trains then negotiate a series of turns and four heart-roll inversions before dropping 80 feet to the ride's conclusion.

Since its opening in 1992, Hurricane Reef had become increasingly crowded. As a result, in 1999 it was decided to double the size of the facility, transforming it into an all new water park—WaterWorks. A passageway was built underneath the Rebel Yell, opening up nine wooded acres to accommodate three new attractions. This includes a 650,000-gallon wave pool; the Surf City Splash House, a 40-foot-tall play area with fifty interactive elements including a giant bucket that would occasionally tip over drenching everyone below; and Lil' Barefoot Beach, a play area for smaller children. The following season, Pipeline Peak opened in the new area. A 77-foot-tall tower, Pipeline Peak features four waterslides including the Night Slider, a 77-foot speed slide; Power Plunge, a twisting body slide; Turbo Twister, a 45-foot-high, two-person tube slide; and Riptide, a 495-foot-long two-person inner tube slide.

Pipeline Peak is one of the many water slides that can be enjoyed in the Water-Works water park.

Hypersonic XLC broke new ground when it opened in 2001 as the first compressed air-launched roller coaster.

Nickelodeon Central also opened in 2000. An expansion of Splat City, it added a Nickelodeon-themed show and two rides—the Space Surfer, which gives riders a chance to pilot their own planes high in the sky, and the Rugrats Toontike, a car ride for small children.

The park decided it was time to step up in the roller coaster sweepstakes in 2001 when it broke new ground with the installation of Hyper-Sonic XLC. Like its predecessors, HyperSonic again utilized a launch system rather than a traditional lift hill. Built by S&S Power, it is the world's first air-launched roller coaster, using compressed air to accelerate the train from 0 to 80 miles per hour in 1.8 seconds. The train then ascends a 165-foot-tall tower straight up, then straight down before returning to the station.

The concept for the 1,560-foot-long roller coaster was created by S&S president Stan Checketts when he was traversing a near-vertical hill on one of his souped-up, custom-designed snowmobiles. Checketts thought that the popular compressed-air launch system that he perfected for drop towers could also provide an excellent means to propel a roller coaster train up and over a vertical hill. The result was HyperSonic XLC (for extreme launched coaster). He first erected the ride at his factory in Logan, Utah, and after fine-tuning, shipped it to Virginia on over sixty trucks.

The Daring Dozen

Kings Dominion was promoting the "Daring Dozen" the next year when it opened its twelfth roller coaster. Ricochet was a departure from the park's other recent roller coaster additions as it was a family ride rather than an intense thriller, but it was again a product of the latest roller coaster renaissance. Ricochet is a wild-mouse-style roller coaster, which uses sharp turns rather than steep drops as its primary thrill element. Wild Mouse roller coasters originally debuted in the late 1950s and enjoyed a surge of popularity through the early 1960s before they were supplanted by other rides. In the 1990s, however, roller coaster designers again looked to these designs to create a new generation of Wild Mouse roller coasters. Kings Dominion's model was built by Mack of Germany and stands 52 feet tall with 1,340 feet of track.

Since opening, the Eiffel Tower had dominated the skyline as Kings Dominion's tallest structure. In 2003, however, it gained a neighbor when the 305-foot-tall Drop Zone: Stunt Tower opened. Nearly twice the height of any of the other thrill rides in the park, Drop Zone features a massive ride vehicle, seating fifty-six people around the central tower, which is hauled to the top. It is then released for a 272-foot free fall at speeds of 73 miles per hour before being brought to a stop by special magnetic brakes.

Expansion continued over the next few seasons with Scooby Doo and the Haunted Mansion, an interactive dark ride that opened in 2004, and Tomb Raider: Firefall, a themed flipping-top spin ride that debuted in 2005.

The roller coaster lineup expanded to a "baker's dozen" in 2006 with the addition of The Italian Job Turbo Coaster. The ride represented a departure from past roller coasters as it eschewed record-challenging thrills for a complete ride experience. On The Italian Job Turbo Coaster, passengers board

The Eiffel Tower gained a neighbor on the skyline when Drop Zone: Stunt Tower opened in 2003.

replicas of Mini Cooper S cars. Linear induction motors launch the trains out of the station at 40 miles per hour into a tight 45-foot-tall spiral. From there the riders experience a series of near collisions; race down "stairs," through tunnels; escape explosions; and are even menaced by a helicopter all in just 1,960 feet of track. Premier Rides of Millersville, Maryland, developed the ride system, although the concept was created by Paramount Parks' design group.

It was ironic that such an elaborately themed ride would debut the same season that Paramount, which was now part of Viacom, decided to sell its theme park division. After several months, CedarFair, LP, emerged as the winner in a $1.24 billion deal. CedarFair is a publicly held company that achieved fame by purchasing Cedar Point, a dying amusement park in Sandusky, Ohio, in 1956 and transforming it into the largest and arguably most successful amusement resort in the Midwest. As Cedar Point grew to dominate its market, CedarFair launched an acquisition spree that added parks in Minnesota, Pennsylvania, and Missouri, along with Knott's Berry Farm in California. With the acquisition of Kings Dominion and its four sister parks in California, North Carolina, Ohio, and Canada, CedarFair became a $1 billion company and a dominant force in the theme park industry.

For 2007, its first full season under its new owners, Kings Dominion returned to WaterWorks for another major expansion. Among the new features are Tidal Wave Bay, a second wave pool; the Zoom Flume family raft slide; and the Tornado, a 65-foot-tall waterslide.

The look of International Street was dramatically changed in 2008 when Dominator debuted next to Berserker. Taking HyperSonic's place among the park's roller coaster lineup, Dominator was relocated from Geauga Lake, Aurora, Ohio, where it first opened in 2000. The ride is one of the largest roller coasters to ever be moved, standing 161 feet tall with a 157 foot drop and 4,210 feet of track. Other features on this massive ride include a 135 foot tall vertical loop, four additional inversions and unique "floorless trains".

Kings Dominion Today

Kings Dominion continues to embrace the spectacular scale in which it was built, having grown into one of the largest theme parks in the country featuring over forty rides, a water park with seventeen waterslides, two wave pools, two play areas, and a lazy river; live shows; and a variety of other attractions.

International Street serves as the park's grand entryway. A promenade over 300 feet long with shops surrounding a grand fountain is all overseen by the 330-foot-tall Eiffel Tower. The Eiffel Tower serves as the park's main hub and provides access to most of the other areas of the park including Nickelodeon Central, KidZville, The Grove, and Old Virginia.

The wooded Old Virginia is home to the Shenandoah Lumber Company log flume, the White Water Canyon river rapids, the Blue Ridge Tollway, the Grizzly wooden roller coaster, and the Flying Eagles, a classic flying scooter ride where riders can pilot their own plane. Old Virginia leads to The Grove, Kings Dominion's largest area and home to five of the park's roller coasters including the twin-track Rebel Yell, hilly Hurler, twisting Ricochet, and stand-up Shockwave. Other rides include the 305-foot-tall Drop Zone: Stunt Tower and the classic hand-carved carousel.

The entrance to WaterWorks, Kings Dominion's water park, is near Drop Zone. The water park is divided into two large sections. Closest to the entrance are four waterslide towers and the Lazy Rider river attraction. A passageway leads through the Rebel Yell and into the woods where guests will find three more waterslide towers, the wave pools, and the water play areas.

The Congo is at the other end of The Grove. Dominated by the 170-foot-tall mountain that houses Volcano, The Blast Coaster, the Congo is also the location of the Anaconda looping roller coaster, Avalanche bobsled coaster, the Flight of Fear indoor coaster, and The Italian Job Turbo Coaster.

Next is KidZville, a sprawling area for children and their families. In addition to ten kiddie rides are two roller coasters, including the wooden Scooby's Ghoster Coaster; Scooby Doo and the Haunted Mansion, an interactive dark ride; the Treasure Cave walk-through; and the Kidz Construction Company play area. Nickelodeon Central rounds out the themed areas offering character meet-and-greet areas, the Green Slime Zone play area, and the Rugrats Toontike where small kids can drive their own cars.

Six Flags America

OPENED 1974

LIKE PEOPLE, AMUSEMENT PARKS CAN SOMETIMES BE LATE BLOOMERS, spending years struggling with their identity and constantly shifting strategies before finding their place in life. Six Flags America is one such park. For nearly twenty years, it could not quite figure out what it wanted to be. But once it did, the story only got better.

A Tough Start

In the late 1960s and early 1970s, one of the concepts being tested in the nascent theme park industry was drive-through animal attractions. Many business people thought the idea of driving through a preserve and seeing animals in natural settings up close from the comfort of one's own vehicle would be a successful idea. Parks began opening throughout the country.

In 1973, Texas billionaire H. Ross Perot teamed up with a pair of Irish animal trainers to propose an animal park on more than 400 acres of corn and tobacco fields just east of Washington, D.C. ABC Television, like many major corporations at the time, was seeking to diversify its holdings and cash in on the theme park boom. It soon bought out Perot and his partners. The planned park joined Silver Springs and Weeki Wachee, two nature-oriented attractions in Florida, and the Historic Towne of Smithville, a historic village near Atlantic City, New Jersey, as the basis of ABC's Scenic and Wildlife Attractions division.

In July 1974, the ABC Wildlife Preserve opened for business. Built at a cost of $17 million, the 400-

Six Flags America
P.O. Box 4210
Largo, MD 20775
301-249-1500
www.sixflags.com/
parks/america/

acre facility featured over 500 animals freely roaming in 280 acres of natural settings that visitors could enjoy from their own vehicles. Given its location in the densely populated northeastern corridor of the country, ABC had high hopes for its success, projecting 850,000 visitors that first season.

Unfortunately, like most similar facilities, the ABC Wildlife Preserve had trouble attracting repeat visitors and attendance fell far short. As one industry observer quipped at the time, "Who wants to see a lion yawn twice?"

Despite the tough first season, ABC went into the second year with a full slate of improvements in hopes of turning things around. An additional $3 million was invested to install an Australian Preserve featuring animals from Down Under, an artisan village, additional theming, and a series of live shows. In addition, the drive-through safari was replaced with Jungle Rovers—four car trams, each holding 130 people, that took passengers on a narrated tour of the preserve.

Yet again, the park could just not gain any momentum and attendance was half the season's projection of 1 million. ABC realized that the Wildlife Preserve could not go on in its current format. Half of the employees were dismissed and the company took a $10 million write-down on its investment.

Briefly, ABC considered expanding the operation into a full-scale theme park at a cost of up to $50 million. As proposed, the park would be called American Adventure and feature sections depicting life in the Yukon, the United States, and Central and South America. But those plans were soon abandoned, as it was decided the investment could not be justified. ABC began searching for a new operator.

In November 1978, things began to look up for the struggling facility when a group headed by naturalist Jim Fowler, best-known as a host on the Wild Kingdom television program, took over the now shuttered park for $3 million. The new owners brought in 521 new animals and spent $1 million to renovate the existing facility. They had ambitious plans to add new animal exhibits designed by Fowler that were intended to get visitors as close to the animals as possible. Also planned was a large monkey playground with a matching children's playground, an eagle aviary, and a large petting zoo.

But again, high hopes failed to generate sufficient business. The renovations never took place, and by 1981 Jim Fowler's Wild Country, as it was then called, was used for little more than the occasional group outing.

A Wild New Beginning

In August 1981, the struggling facility was acquired by Wild World Holdings, comprising a group of seven local businessmen. They saw the potential in operating a theme park in the area, but knew to succeed

LOCATION

Six Flags America is located on Central Avenue, approximately 5 miles east of exit 15A off Interstate 495. The park is also accessible via public transportation. Take the Metro Blue Line toward Largo Town Center and exit at Addison Road. Transfer to the C21 Bus and exit in front of Six Flags America.

OPERATING SCHEDULE

Six Flags America is open weekends in April and May, daily from Memorial Day weekend through late August, during Labor Day weekend, and weekends in October for the Fright Fest Halloween promotion. The park is closed for private events most weekends in September. Check with the park before visiting. During most of the season, the park opens at 10:30 A.M. with closing time varying from 6 to 9 P.M., depending on the time of year.

ADMISSION

A pay-one-price admission of under $50 entitles visitors to all rides and attractions with the exception of games and attractions such as the Sky Coaster and the Sonora Speedway go-carts. Parking is an extra fee. Discounted tickets can be purchased via the Internet on the park's website.

FOOD

Six Flags America features nearly four dozen food outlets ranging from portable carts to indoor restaurants. The Heritage House food court in Olde Boston is a great place to go for families who can't quite figure out what they want, offering hot dogs, pizza, chicken, gyros, and fries. Hollywood Café in Looney Tunes Movie Town features burgers and chicken in air-conditioned comfort. The Crazy Horse Saloon in Coyote Creek serves fried chicken, barbecue sandwiches, and salads, and the Lucky Albatross in Skull Island has burgers and chicken tenders. Kid's meals are available at a number of outlets including the Hollywood Café, the Lucky Albatross, and the Crazy Horse Saloon. There are also a number of franchised outlets in the park including Papa John's pizza, Panda Express, Subway, and Ben and Jerry's.

FOR CHILDREN

Looney Tunes Movie Town is the main kiddie area featuring eleven rides, most of which can be enjoyed by the entire family including the Great Chase roller coaster and the Prop Warehouse play area.

The park also has a number of other rides and attractions for the entire family including the merry-go-round, the Around the World in 80 Days Ferris wheel, and the Great Race car ride.

Hurricane Harbor offers two play areas—Buccaneer Beach and Crocodile Cal's—that are great places for kids to splash around in. The Bamboo Chute slides are also specially built for younger visitors.

(continued on page 126)

VISITING (continued from page 125)

SPECIAL FEATURES

Six Flags America features one of the most diverse collections of roller coasters around. The Wild One is a classic wooden out-and-back ride that began life in 1917 at Paragon Park in Hull, Massachusetts, making it one of the few wooden roller coasters to be successfully relocated to another location. Roar, the park's other wooden roller coaster, looks to the twisting creations of the 1920s for its inspiration. Batwing features unique cars that allow riders to achieve the sensation of flight. Superman—Ride of Steel is the park's flagship ride and at 197 feet is one of the tallest roller coasters on the East Coast. With a top speed of 73 miles per hour and an abundance of negative gs, it provides one of the most thrilling rides around.

Six Flags America's merry-go-round is a one-of-a-kind creation. Unlike most merry-go-rounds, Six Flags America's has no horses, but rather, features a collection of sixty jungle animals.

TIME REQUIRED

Plan to spend at least one full day at Six Flags America, with a second day being optimal. If you are pressed for time and visit on a day when crowds are light, the major attractions can be enjoyed in about six hours.

TOURING TIPS

Purchase your ticket online ahead of time on the park's website. Not only will you be able to avoid lines at the front gate, but Six Flags America offers special online-only discounts.

Try to visit Six Flags America on a weekday when the park tends to be less crowded.

Arrive just before the park opens and try to hit the Gotham City–themed area first to get in its three big roller coasters before the crowd reaches that area.

Throughout the park several locations sell cups that are good for unlimited drink refills for the duration of your visit.

they would have to dramatically expand the scope of the park beyond its animal exhibits.

The new owners launched an $11 million expansion developing the park into Wild World, a multifaceted attraction that would have something for almost everyone. The park acquired six rides from International Amusement Devices, a manufacturer and distributor based in Sandusky, Ohio. These included an Enterprise, a Round Up, the one-of-a-kind All Around, two kiddie rides, and a unique merry-go-round measuring 52 feet in diameter with sixty jungle animals.

The kiddie rides formed the basis of Kiddie City, which also featured a video arcade, a toy shop, games, a puppet show, and a petting zoo. A second kiddie area, called Playport, was anchored by the USS *High and*

Dry, a boat-shaped play structure measuring 30 by 80 feet with several play elements such as a net climb, tunnels, and slides. Also nearby were the Bounce Back, the Boppity Bags, the Ball Bath, the King of the Mountain, and the Get Lost Maze.

Water Works, a water park, was anchored by Rainbow Zoom, a complex of four twisting flumes; Sunstreaker with two 220-foot-long speed slides; and Tadpool, a 10,000-square-foot play area for kids.

The animal attractions were upgraded into Animal Kingdom. A train was installed to take visitors through animal habitats populated by over 300 creatures, and a deer petting area and a live elephant ride were added.

Rounding out the attractions lineup were six shows including magic, country western, live birds and reptiles, and the Cinema 180.

Wild World opened to a crowd of 3,500 people on June 26, 1982, and by the end of what was meant to be a low-key season to test the market, 400,000 had come through the gates. It looked like the park had found its niche.

The next year, the owners followed up with another $5 million in improvements. In the water park, a 45,000-square-foot, 1-million-gallon wave pool was added, and four new rides were installed—the High Seas swinging ship; the Curling Dervish, a high-speed bobsled ride; the Pirate's Flight, a circular ride; and an antique car ride. But while attendance grew to 580,000, it fell well short of the goal of 1.06 million the park had set.

The former ABC Wildlife Preserve reopened as Wild World in 1982. SIX FLAGS AMERICA

As a result, the park undertook a major restructuring to cut expenses. The animals continued to be a costly proposition that was not drawing many people to the facility, so at the end of the season they were sold. As a result Wild World was able to cut $5 million in expenses from its budget.

In addition, the park decided to focus on its water attractions, and placed all but three of the major rides—the High Seas, the Sky Escaper, and the Curling Dervish—into storage. Another $750,000 was invested on improvements including $500,000 to add the Rampage, a 35-foot-tall twin waterslide in which riders on sleds travel down into a 120-foot-long pool. In addition, the Serpentorium, a reptile exhibit, was demolished to make room for a 500-seat water stadium for a high-dive show, and an existing 500-seat theater was equipped with a projector to become the first attraction geared solely to showing promotional music videos, a cutting-edge concept at the time.

"We're the prototype of the new urban eighties park" operations manager Michael Gates said at the time to *Amusement Business* magazine. "We've got to be smaller and more efficient to serve a tighter marketing base than most of these huge theme parks."

The changes failed to resonate with the public and attendance that season plunged to 350,000. Fortunately, new management was brought in to turn around the struggling facility. The new managers noticed that the lack of dry rides hurt attendance on days when the weather was cool, so they brought back most of the rides that had been mothballed a year earlier and added four new kiddie rides. Attendance rebounded and Wild World began searching for a landmark attraction to anchor the park.

A large roller coaster seemed to be the natural addition. But since it was still not thriving financially, Wild World needed a cost-effective solution. The owners approached Charlie Dinn, the leading builder of wooden roller coasters in the 1980s, about the feasibility of moving a wooden roller coaster to the park. He initially was hesitant and recommended building a new version of the Shooting Star, a long-gone ride from Coney Island in Cincinnati, Ohio, where Dinn started his career in the 1960s. He had a change of heart in 1985, however, when he was involved in the successful relocation of a wooden roller coaster to Knoebels Amusement Resort in Elysburg, Pennsylvania.

About that time, Paragon Park, which had closed after the 1984 season to make way for a condominium development, was making plans to sell off its rides. The park's feature attraction was the Giant Coaster, a highly regarded 98-foot-tall, 3,300-foot-long wooden roller coaster. It was originally erected in 1917 and had entertained 15 million riders during its time in Massachusetts. Initially, Dinn was not sure it would be a good candidate for relocation as it was not in the best of shape, but he was familiar with the ride, having worked on it in the past, and it had a reputation as a great ride.

As a result, Wild World approached Paragon Park about the possibility of giving it the ride, thinking Paragon would save on demolition costs. But Paragon insisted on including it in the auction of the park's assets. On June 12, 1985, with a winning bid of $28,000, Wild World became the proud owner of the Giant Coaster.

By mid-October, Dinn was leading a crew of sixteen people in dismantling the ride and shipping it down to Maryland on twelve flatbed trucks. Work proceeded through the winter, and over a three-month period, the ride slowly came to life on a portion of the former wildlife area.

Wild World was not content to rebuild the ride as it was. In 1963, a fire had destroyed a spiraling turn at the end of the Giant Coaster and budget constraints at Paragon Park had precluded its re-erection. Wild World, however, wanted to make the ride complete and built a new 540-degree helix. Since blueprints of the original did not exist, Dinn used an old postcard of the Giant Coaster to duplicate it. The new helix added 700 feet to the length of the ride, increasing it to 4,000 feet. In the end, although Wild World replaced 75 percent of the original lumber, the total cost to construct the renamed Wild One was just $1 million. To build a similar ride new would have cost $2.5 million.

The story of the relocation of the Giant Coaster and its rebirth generated national publicity for the park. In fact, a wedding on the Wild One on June 7 received coverage from *Entertainment Tonight* and *Good Morning America*. The Wild One, however, was not the only new addition that season. So the little ones would not be left out, Wild World also added the Cannonball, a 12-foot-tall kiddie coaster.

The opening of the Wild One helped to generate a 12 percent increase in attendance for Wild World. The park again seemed to be on track, and it followed up in 1987 with a major expansion of the water park in the form of Paradise

The 1986 relocation of the Giant Coaster from Massachusetts to Wild World put the park on the roller coaster map. AUGIE GEIST

Paradise Island dramatically expanded the water park when it opened in 1987.

Island. Containing a half million gallons of water, the area featured a 30,000-square-foot activity pool with six waterslides and other play elements, along with a 750-foot-long lazy river.

The 1988 season saw $1.5 million in improvements, primarily upgrading park infrastructure, although a tilt-a-whirl ride joined the lineup. The next season the Playport kiddie area was removed and replaced by Rafters Run, a 57-foot-tall twin waterslide featuring 460 feet of twists and turns and a 150-foot tunnel. By now, Wild World seemed to be on a roll. Attendance had increased to a record 600,000, and the park had put together a well-balanced mix of attractions.

Premiering a New Era

Unfortunately, by 1991 Wild World's outlook had changed dramatically. Competition had increased, deferred maintenance was catching up with the facility, the buildings were looking dated, and the owners were falling behind in taxes and loans and were being sued for nonpayment of bills. Because of a zoning dispute and maintenance needs, the Wild One did not even open for the season. Attendance dropped to 387,000 and Wild World was put up for sale.

Fortunately, by December the struggling facility had caught the attention of Premier Parks, Incorporated, of Oklahoma City. Premier Parks got its start in 1981 when the company, then known as Tierco, purchased Frontier City, a run-down amusement park in Oklahoma City. The original intent was to redevelop the park for other uses, but when the economy in Oklahoma took a downturn, Tierco found itself in the amusement park business. It renovated Frontier City and upon seeing the increase in business that resulted, decided to expand the company. Tierco soon purchased a water park in Oklahoma City and went shopping for other acquisitions. Wild World was the type of facility they wanted—a mid-sized amusement park in a solid market that needed an infusion of capital and management.

On January 14, 1992, Premier Parks closed the deal to purchase Wild World for $5 million plus a settlement of a $9 million lawsuit brought against the former owners by the Federal Deposit Insurance Corporation over a disputed loan. Since the deal closed just seven weeks prior to the start of the season, Premier was rather limited in the improvements it could make, but it also knew it was important to show that the park was on the upswing. As a result, Premier launched an $800,000 overhaul of the park.

Premier identified several critical areas for improvement. With only nine major rides, there was a limited selection of attractions outside the water park. The water park, the biggest draw, was an unappealing sea of concrete. The park's aesthetics were outdated, having been changed little in the past decade; and most critically, its flagship attraction, the Wild One, was inoperable.

As a result, in the limited time available, Premier added a bumper car ride, four kiddie rides and five new live shows. It also launched a $500,000 rehabilitation of the water park, rebranding it as Paradise Island, expanding the Tadpool, and giving the 25-acre area a tropical theme with hundreds of palm and banana trees and thatching on the roofs of buildings. In addition, distinctive facades were added to plain-looking buildings, landscaping was upgraded, and veteran roller coaster builder John F. Pierce was hired to perform $250,000 in renovations on the Wild One.

But Premier saw a much greater opportunity for Wild World—given that 6 million people lived within 50 miles of the park—than the previous owners had. As a result, with a full season to plan, the company launched a $5.9 million expansion for the 1993 season focusing on the amusement park side of the operation by adding six major rides. The largest attraction was the Python, a looping roller coaster. Acquired from Six Flags Great Adventure, Jackson, New Jersey, Python was a shuttle loop roller coaster in which riders climb to the top of a 56-tall-tower where they board the train. The train is then launched from the station, and plunges down a 47-foot drop at 45 miles per hour and through a vertical loop. After climbing back up another hill the ride is launched backward through the loop and into the station.

Python was the first roller coaster added by Premier Parks when the company acquired Wild World. SIX FLAGS AMERICA

Replacing the Rampage waterslide was Shipwreck Falls, a 50-foot-tall, 760-foot-long splashwater ride in which boats plunge down a 45-foot drop creating a huge wave that drenches riders and watchers alike. Other new major rides included the Great Race antique car ride; the Cyclone, a scrambler ride; a Ferris wheel, which made a one-year appearance in honor of the 100th anniversary of the invention of the classic ride; and the Falling Star. The Falling Star had been originally ordered by pop star Michael Jackson for his personal amusement park, but he later changed his mind sending Chance Rides, the manufacturer, searching for a new buyer.

Younger visitors also received an all new kiddie area—A Day at the Circus. All but two of the kiddie rides, the Ferris wheel and the Cannonball roller coaster, were removed and replaced by ten new kiddie and family rides including bumper cars, bumper boats, a balloon ride, spinning tubs, flying elephants, swings, a train, and a miniature merry-go-round. Completing the area were two shows and the Clown Town climbing complex. Rounding out the ambitious improvement program was a new front gate area.

Living the Adventure

The 1993 expansion was very well received, with attendance jumping 44 percent over 1992 levels. But Premier Parks was not done yet, budgeting $8.5 million for improvements for 1994. To accommodate the increasing crowds, Coyote Creek, an all new 10-acre Wild West–themed area was constructed complete with a general store, an ice cream parlor, a candy shop, a photo gallery, an arcade, and a $1 million Wild West stunt show. Rides included bumper cars and Renegade Rapids, a trip down a 1,350-foot-long white-water river.

Additions elsewhere in the park included the Iron Eagle, an 82-foot-tall ride that rotated 360 degrees on its axis, while spinning forty-two passengers upside down; a Flying Carousel swing ride; spinning Tea Cups; a balloon-themed Ferris wheel; and the Black Hole, a dual speed slide that replaced the Sunstreaker in Paradise Island.

Given the improvements it had made, Premier no longer thought that Wild World accurately reflected what the park had become and changed the facility's name to Adventure World. "We wanted to have enough critical mass behind it before changing the name," Premier CEO Gary Story told *Fun World* magazine, explaining the name came from the desire to have people to associate the park with a family adventure. Again, attendance jumped by 19 percent.

The park had finally seemed to find its way. But Adventure World was not about to rest on its laurels. The 1995 season saw the addition of the Mind Eraser, a $7 million inverted roller coaster in Coyote Creek built by Vekoma International of the Netherlands. Standing 109 feet tall, the 2,260-foot-long ride takes riders through five inversions at speeds of up to 50 miles per hour, while riders sit in trains suspended

Mind Eraser was representative of a new generation of inverted roller coasters.

underneath the track. By now attendance had reached 725,000, double the level recorded in 1992.

The park reached new heights the following season with the addition of the $4 million Tower of Doom, a new generation free fall ride from the Swiss manufacturer Intamin. Riders take four-person cars to the top of a 140-foot-tall tower and free fall for 100 feet at 56 miles per hour, only to be stopped by magnetic brakes. Joining Tower of Doom was an 880-foot-long go-cart track, along with the Crazy Horse Saloon in Coyote Creek.

Adventure World set new records in 1997 with $14 million in improvements. At the heart of the expansion that season was Skull Island, a 10-acre pirate-themed area next to Coyote Creek. Anchoring the area is Skull Mountain, a one-of-a-kind, $12 million flume ride. Billed as the "21st century mating of the log flume and roller coaster," the 2,200-foot-long ride begins with a 30-foot incline. At the top, the boats are spun around 150 degrees and then travel backward through a camel hump chute section. They are then rotated again for a climb up a 60-foot hill for the final splashdown through the mouth of a giant skull. Joining Skull Mountain were a pirate stunt show, shops, a food court, and the existing High Seas and Pirate's Flight rides.

The park grew dramatically during the 1990s during its transformation from Wild World to Adventure World.

Roar is based on the twisting roller coaster designs of the 1920s.

Along with the addition of the Skull Island area, the water park received Crocodile Cal's Outback Beach House, a 24,000-square-foot play area. It is anchored by a five-story interactive tree house with 100 water-powered play features including a 1,000-gallon bucket, water mines, geysers, shower bursts, water guns, pump guns, and hose jets.

With attendance now nearing 1 million people annually, Adventure World saw the need for another roller coaster to complement its existing lineup. At that time, a new company, Great Coasters International of Sunbury, Pennsylvania, caught the attention of the industry with its modern versions of the classic wooden twisting coasters of the 1920s. Adventure World knew that such a design would be the perfect partner to Wild One's straighter out-and-back-style layout. The result was Roar, a twisting wooden ride standing 90 feet tall and reaching speeds of up to 50 miles per hour on 3,200 feet of track. A key part of the ride's appeal is its fifteen curves, fourteen drops, and twenty track crossovers. "It was the trickiest design I ever worked on," designer Mike Boodley told trade publication *Amusement Today*. "It's complicated and the layout is extremely tight." The public must have liked Roar as Adventure World's attendance topped 1 million for the first time.

Raising the Flags

By the end of 1998, Premier Parks had spent over $40 million improving Adventure World. Attendance had tripled, and the park had established itself as a major destination in the Washington-Baltimore area; but an event that occurred earlier in the year would have a profound effect on its future. Since the purchase of Adventure World, Premier Parks continued to make acquisitions and had emerged as the third largest amusement park chain in the United States with thirteen parks throughout the country. In February 1998, Premier Parks stunned the industry by announcing that it would acquire the nation's second largest amusement park operator, Six Flags Theme Parks.

Six Flags' origins date back to 1961 when Texas real estate developer Angus Wynne opened a theme park to anchor the Great Southwest Industrial District, a 5,000-acre development located in Arlington, Texas. During this period, developers throughout the United States were trying to duplicate the success of Disneyland, which changed the industry when it opened in 1955. All previous attempts had failed.

The park's six areas were themed after the countries of which Texas had once been a part—the Confederacy, France, Mexico, Spain, Texas, and the United States—leading to the name Six Flags Over Texas. By pioneering concepts such as the pay-one-price admission and introducing rides such as the Runaway Mine Train and the Log Flume, Six Flags Over Texas succeeded where others had failed. Soon the concept was expanded to new Six Flags theme parks in Atlanta and St. Louis.

Throughout the 1970s and 1980s, Six Flags expanded by acquiring parks throughout the United States. In 1985, the Looney Tunes characters such as Bugs Bunny and Daffy Duck became the chain's official ambassadors.

By the time Six Flags was acquired by Premier Parks, it had established itself as an operator of cutting-edge thrill rides. Premier, which would soon be renamed Six Flags, Incorporated, knew that several of its existing parks had grown enough under their management to warrant conversion to the better known Six Flags format.

In October 1998, the company announced that Adventure World, along with sister parks in California, Colorado, Kentucky, and New York would become Six Flags theme parks, joining seventeen others in the chain. The switch would involve infrastructure improvements, thrill ride additions, and the introduction of the famous Looney Tunes characters, a Six Flags staple.

Through the winter and spring of 1999, workers scrambled to transform Adventure World into Six Flags America, undertaking $40 million in improvements that left few areas of the park untouched.

The entrance area was transformed into Main Street 1776, complete with Georgian architecture and a street of Colonial-themed shops and food stands. A Day at the Circus was transformed into the Looney Tunes Movie Town, home to the famous cartoon characters. The Clown Town climbing complex and a half dozen of the older kiddie rides, including the Cannonball Coaster, were removed. In their place were five new family rides including the Great Chase, a 10-foot-tall, 280-foot-long family roller coaster; Bugs Bunny's Back Lot Trucking Company; and Daffy's Movie Town Tours crazy bus. Also added was the Prop Warehouse and an enclosed, interactive play area featuring slides, tunnels, mazes, and thousands of foam balls. The six rides retained were all rethemed to various Looney Tunes characters.

Nearby, the Python roller coaster was removed to make way for Two-Face: The Flip Side, a 161-foot-tall steel roller coaster from Vekoma International. On Two-Face, riders sit face-to-face in cars suspended underneath the 1,014-foot-long track. The train is pulled up a 137-foot lift and dropped. It then flies 55 miles per hour back down the lift, shooting up into a double inversion boomerang, then into a 72-foot-high vertical loop before rushing to the top of a second 137-foot lift. Riders have just enough time to catch their breath before the coaster train is released, propelling them through the entire ride again in the opposite direction.

Behind the Wild One, which underwent a $1 million renovation, a new 6-acre Gotham City–themed area was added where the wild animals once roamed. Home to the DC Comics characters, Gotham City was dominated by Joker's Jinx, a unique steel roller coaster designed by Premier Rides of nearby Millersville, Maryland. Doing away with the traditional lift hill, the ride uses forty-four linear induction motors arrayed along a 200-foot-long stretch of track to catapult a 9-ton train from 0 to 63 miles per hour in less than four seconds.

The train then travels through a 79-foot-tall jumble of track that features thirty vertical curves, twenty-five horizontal curves, and four inver-

Main Street 1776 was a new entrance area added to the park during its transformation to Six Flags America in 1999.

sions. Each launch requires 7,000 amps of electricity for four seconds, the equivalent of adding a large shopping mall to the power grid. As a result the addition of Joker's Jinx required special power storage capacitors.

Gotham City's other major new attraction was the Batman Thrill Spectacular, a new stunt show where guests are placed into a set of a Batman movie, with the Caped Crusader's battles against his enemies highlighted by challenging stunts and mind-blowing pyrotechnics. In fact the flames in the show are so intense that they require four 1,000-gallon propane tanks.

Rounding out the additions for the year was the Rodeo, a high-speed spinning ride in Coyote Creek. The former Wildlife Preserve had finally hit the big time and the public responded with a 59 percent increase in attendance to a record 1.7 million.

Six Flags America was determined to keep the positive momentum going in 2000 following up with its largest ride ever. Superman—Ride Of Steel is a hypercoaster, a type of steel roller coaster that emphasizes high speeds and large drops rather than loops. Built by Intamin of Switzerland, the $15 million, 5-million-pound ride stands 197 feet tall and features a 205-foot drop at speeds of up to 73 miles per hour along its 5,350 feet of steel track. Opening Superman were twenty hometown heroes, winners of a local essay contest.

In addition to the roller coaster, Six Flags also added three new spinning rides that season—the Octopus, the Alpine Bobs, and the Krypton Comet—to help handle growing crowds.

As if four new roller coasters in two years were not enough, Six Flags followed up in 2001 with Batwing. Batwing is another unique roller

Superman—Ride of Steel and Joker's Jinx are two of the roller coasters found in the park's Gotham City area.

Batwing is a unique roller coaster in which riders "fly" beneath the tracks.

coaster from Vekoma featuring trains that allow riders to "fly" through the air. Visitors are secured in twenty-four-person trains facing backward. As the train leaves the station, riders are tilted back so they are lying down facing the sky as they climb a 115-foot-tall lift hill. At the top of the lift, the train flips over, putting riders into a flying position to soar through five inversions along its 3,340 feet of track.

After focusing on roller coasters for so many years, Six Flags moved in a new direction in 2003 with the addition of Penguin's Blizzard River. Designed and manufactured by Whitewater West Industries of Canada, the 60-foot-tall, 669-foot-long water ride hauls riders in six-person rafts to the top of a 60-foot-tall hill where they then are sent down a twisting flume. With rafts spinning, they travel through two megatwists and a triple-dip drop culminating in a splashdown that includes a series of geyser blasts. Onlookers can participate by firing water cannons at rafts as they land in the bay.

Since the conversion to Six Flags, the Paradise Island water park had been the only major area in the park not to see any significant improvements. As a result, Six Flags America launched the largest expansion in its history for the 2005 season, converting Paradise Island into Six Flags Hurricane Harbor.

The entire area received a Caribbean-themed makeover. The Kids Cove area was transformed into an all new attraction, Buccaneer Beach, expanding it from 6,500 to 10,500 square feet and adding slides, palm trees, and a pirate ship. In addition, two new water attractions were constructed. The Tornado resembles an enormous 60-foot-tall, 60-foot-in-diameter funnel turned on its side. From a height of 75 feet, it carries four riders in cloverleaf-shaped tubes down a 132-foot-long tunnel into the funnel splashing back and forth on 5,000 gallons of swirling water. Nearby, the 55-foot-tall Bahama Blast sends four passenger tubes down a 517-foot-long twisting triple-dip course through a tunnel.

Six Flags America Today

Despite its troubled beginning, Six Flags America has grown into one of the largest theme parks in the eastern United States, featuring more than forty rides, including eight roller coasters, a water park with more than a dozen attractions, and over a half-dozen live shows.

Visitors are greeted by the elaborate colonial-themed main entrance that leads to the Main Street 1776 area, home to several shops, eateries, and services. At the end of Main Street 1776 is the entrance to Hurricane Harbor. Entering this large water park, guests come upon the Hurricane Mountain waterslides, Buccaneer Beach kids play area, and Hurricane Bay wave pool. Next to the wave pool is the Castaway Creek lazy river, along with several smaller waterslides and play elements. The largest slides come next including the Mako and the Hammerhead speed slides, the Tornado, and the Bahama Blast. The Crocodile Cal's Caribbean Beach House water play area rounds out the attractions.

Back in the theme park, Main Street 1776 leads to the Olde Boston themed area. Shaded under tall trees, this area is home to the Around the World in 80 Days Ferris wheel, the Flying Carousel, the Tea Cups, and the unique horseless merry-go-round. A number of food stands are also in this area. Olde Boston leads to Looney Tunes Movie Town, the sprawling kiddie area with eleven rides including the Great Chase roller coaster, along with the Prop Warehouse play area. Movie Town is also the place to meet your favorite Looney Tunes characters.

Southwest Territory is located next to Movie Town and is home to the Wild One and the Two-Face roller coasters, along with the Tower of Doom drop ride. A passageway through the Wild One provides the entrance to Gotham City where guests can be entertained by the Batman Thrill Spectacular show; cool off on Penguin's Blizzard River; be thrown for a loop on the Jokers' Jinx roller coaster; climb to the heavens on Superman—Ride of Steel; or fly above the ground on Batwing.

The Skull Island–themed area is also located near the entrance of Gotham City and is home to the Skull Mountain flume, the Roar wooden roller coaster, and the pirate-themed High Seas, and Pirate's Flight rides. Nantucket is next, where guest can get drenched on Shipwreck Falls.

Coyote Creek is the final area. This elaborately themed western town offers guests a chance to cool off on Renegade Rapids, get thrown for a loop on the Mind Eraser, or enjoy shows in the Crazy Horse Saloon and the Wild West Theater.

Busch Gardens Europe

OPENED 1975

LIKE THE CONTINENT FROM WHICH IT TAKES ITS NAME, BUSCH GARDENS Europe is truly a world apart. Upon arriving, visitors discover that thick trees conceal all but the tallest roller coasters. Guests aren't greeted by a front gate, but rather are transported to another place by a leisurely stroll down a wooded path. But even then, the entrance is quite understated and does little to reveal the delights that await within. Busch Gardens is truly a place like no other.

Creating a Special Place

In the years after World War II, the Anheuser-Busch Company emerged as the largest brewer in the country. In some cases, as it opened new breweries, the company developed small attractions featuring gardens and animal displays to complement the brewery tours offered to the public.

By the early 1970s, the theme park industry was starting to establish itself in the wake of the successful opening of Disneyland and Six Flags Over Texas. Anheuser-Busch decided to launch an analysis of the nine breweries it operated in the United States to see which ones could benefit from the addition of theme parks. Long-established attractions in Tampa, Houston, and Los Angeles were natural candidates and were targeted for expansion. In addition, Busch's newest brewery, in Williamsburg, Virginia, presented a very intriguing opportunity.

The brewery and hospitality center had opened in 1972, occupying just a portion of a 3,600-acre parcel that the company had acquired a few years

Busch Gardens Europe
One Busch Gardens Blvd.
Williamsburg,
Virginia 23187-8785
800-343-7946
www.buschgardens.com/bgw/

earlier. As a result, there was ample room to develop a first-class theme park to complement a housing and resort development planned for the remaining acreage. In addition, over 2 million people lived within 50 miles, 3 million vacationers passed within 50 miles of the site on the way to other destinations, and nearly 1 million people visited nearby Colonial Williamsburg annually. The choice was easy to make and a 360-acre parcel was set aside for the development.

With the decision made to go ahead with the theme park, the next challenge was to develop a concept for the new facility. Since so much American history surrounded the site in the form of Colonial Williamsburg, Jamestown, and Yorktown, Anheuser-Busch sought to differentiate itself by focusing on Europe—the Old Country—as homage to the ancestral homes of many of the people who created this history.

The St. Louis architectural firm of Peckham, Guyton, Albers, and Viets, Incorporated, which continues to be involved with the design of new attractions at the park, was hired to create a series of seven seventeenth-century European hamlets, reflective of England, France, and Germany, nestled among 100 rolling, heavily wooded acres. No detail was spared to transform visitors to another place and another time. The dozen rides, half-dozen live shows, and other attractions were carefully selected to fit in with the theme of each area. Although the park has changed over the past three decades as new attractions and areas were added, nearly all of these hamlets remain almost as they were that first season.

Banbury Cross, now called England, was the entrance area, characterized by authentic English Tudor architecture complete with square-headed nails and oak beams. The main attractions included a Big Ben clock, the Royal Preserve petting zoo, and a 1,000-seat replica of William Shakespeare's Globe Theatre featuring Ghosts of the Globe, a special effects show starring famous Shakespearian characters.

Heatherdowns carried a Scottish theme and is the location of the Highland Stables, home to the famous Budweiser Clydesdales.

Hastings had the look of medieval England complete with an entrance through a castle gate. Attractions included a Sid and Marty Krofft puppet show; the Catapult, an indoor scrambler ride that recreated the Battle of Hastings using sound and lighting effects; and the Turvy Manor fun house.

Aquitane, now called France, carried a French provincial theme complete with winding streets, a sidewalk café, a 1,000-seat theater, and the LeMans auto ride. Nearby were a bird show and a monorail connecting the theme park to the brewery's Hospitality Center.

New France resembled a French trapper's outpost, featuring artisans displaying and selling their wares in log buildings, and Le Scoot, a 1,419-foot-long log flume nestled into a ravine. Built by Arrow Dynamics, one

LOCATION

Located 3 miles east of historic Williamsburg, Virginia; 150 miles from Washington, D.C.; and 50 miles from Richmond and the Norfolk and Virginia Beach resort areas, Busch Gardens Europe is easily accessible off Exit 243A of Interstate 64.

Water Country USA is located 3 miles west of Busch Gardens on State Route 199, a quarter mile from Exit 242B off Interstate 64.

OPERATING SCHEDULE

Busch Gardens Europe kicks off its season the last weekend in March. After being open daily the week before and after Easter, the park is open Friday through Sunday until late May when daily operation commences through Labor Day. Busch Gardens is again open Friday through Sunday through October. The park opens at 10 A.M. all days with closing times varying from 6 P.M. to 11 P.M. depending on the time of year.

Water Country USA opens weekends in mid-May and is open daily from Memorial Day weekend through Labor Day. The park opens at 10 A.M. with closing time ranging between 6 P.M. and 8 P.M.

ADMISSION

Busch Gardens Europe and Water Country USA offer a wide array of admission plans to suit any visitor. One-day admission to Busch Gardens Europe costs under $60 and gives visitors access to all rides, shows, and attractions. Water Country's single-day admission is under $40.

Also available are two-day passes, combination passes with Water Country USA, season passes, and vacation passes, which provide unlimited admission to both Busch Gardens and Water Country USA for up to seven consecutive calendar days.

FOOD

Busch Gardens Europe features over two dozen food outlets ranging from simple stands to restaurants serving authentic European fare. Das Festhaus is the largest facility and is the place to go for authentic German food and deli items. It is a great place to go to eat and take in a show when the weather is inclement. Grogan's Grille in Ireland serves up Irish stew and corned beef, and Trapper's Smokehouse in New France is known for its barbecue. Guests looking for Italian specialties can enjoy live entertainment while they eat at Ristorante della Piazza. Breakfast items are available at The Squire's Grille in England, which also serves burgers, sandwiches, and salads.

Water Country USA has nearly a dozen food outlets, the largest of which include WC's Hot Spot Café for sandwiches; Catalina for pizza, burgers, hot dogs, and chicken tenders; and Daddy O's for pizza, chicken tenders, and nachos.

(continued on page 144)

VISITING (continued from page 143)

FOR CHILDREN

Land of the Dragons is the main kiddie area at Busch Gardens Europe, featuring a wide array of contraptions for kids to play in, five dragon-themed rides including a flume and a Ferris wheel and even a special theater.

Other kiddie rides are scattered throughout the park, particularly in Oktoberfest and Leonardo's Garden of Invention, where one finds the one-of-a-kind hang glider ride. The Lil' Clydes ride in Scotland is another unique kiddie attraction giving children an opportunity to ride on a miniature Clydesdale.

Busch Gardens is also filled with rides the entire family can enjoy including the train, the sky ride, the Kinder Karousel, and the Le Scoot flume. Other attractions kids will love are the animal attractions in Jack Hanna's Wild Reserve and most of the live shows.

At Water Country USA, kids can choose from three play areas including the outer space themed H2O UFO, the whimsical Cow-A-Bunga, and the Kritter Korral for the smallest kids.

SPECIAL FEATURES

There are few theme parks in the world that can rival the beauty, both natural and man-made, of Busch Gardens Europe. Consistently voted the world's most beautiful theme park by the members of the National Amusement Park Historical Association, Busch Gardens features 100 acres of gardens, walkways, and flower beds, including 30,000 plants and flowers grown in a 17,000-square-foot behind-the-scenes greenhouse. Groundskeepers spend six hours daily caring for the plantings.

But the beauty of Busch Gardens is not solely about the landscaping. Each area features some of the most detailed theming anywhere, from the authentic Tudor architecture in England to Germany's Glockenspiel to Roman graffiti on walls in Italy. Keep your eyes open, you'll never know what you are going to find.

The myths and monsters that compose Busch Gardens Europe's roller coaster lineup are hard to beat. For beginners, The Big Bad Wolf offers a free swinging flight through the treetops. The legendary Loch Ness Monster sends riders through a looping journey over the Rhine River, and Alpengeist roars through a ravine with trains traveling beneath the track. Apollo's Chariot is highlighted by its large drops and high speeds, and Griffon offers not one, but two vertical plunges.

There are few rides like Curse of DarKastle, which takes a traditional dark ride several steps further with its cutting-edge combination of motion simulators and special effects.

Escape from Pompeii offers another unique twist on a common theme park attraction, by turning a simple splashwater ride into a journey into the fires of Pompeii.

Lorikeet Glen offers a different-paced attraction to visitors. Guests have the unique opportunity to interact with these friendly birds. One can purchase a cup of nectar and the birds will happily sit on your arm to enjoy it.

Busch Gardens Europe takes great pride in its wide array of high-quality live shows that in many cases transport visitors to another land.

What would a visit to Busch Gardens Europe be without sampling some Anheuser-Busch products? Although they are available at most of the larger food service locations, the best way to do it is to visit the Anheuser-Busch BrewMaster's Club. This unique attraction has locations in Das Festhaus and Ireland that offer a thirty-minute introduction to brewing and enjoying beer. Reservations are recommended.

Busch Entertainment's attention to detail extends to Water Country USA with its 1950s' and 1960s' surf-themed attractions. Aquazoid and Hubba Hubba Highway are two one-of-a-kind water attractions with a variety of special effects and thematic elements.

TIME REQUIRED

Plan on devoting at least one full day to experience Busch Gardens Europe and another for Water Country USA. Combined with nearby Colonial Williamsburg, a trip to Busch Gardens Europe and Water Country USA can easily be a vacation in and of itself.

TOURING TIPS

If you can, visit Busch Gardens Europe on one of the Fridays that the park is open in the spring or fall, or during fall Sundays as those tend to be among the least crowded days. During the summer, weekdays tend to have lighter crowds.

On many days, the England and Scotland areas open earlier than the rest of the park. Start your visit there and make your way to the back of the park, either Oktoberfest or New France, to get a jump on the crowds.

Grogan's Pub is a great place to go on a hot summer day. Enjoy some Anheuser-Busch beverages that are not widely available elsewhere and a basket of pretzels in air-conditioned comfort.

The lunch rush at both facilities is between noon and 2:30 P.M. One can minimize waiting by planning to eat before or after these times.

Crowds at Water Country USA tend to be lightest first thing in the morning or late in the afternoon.

Water Country USA has two changing facilities. The one located closest to the front gate tends to be most crowded, so check out the one next to Cow-A-Bunga.

The pools in Water Country are heated to 82 degrees, so don't let cooler temperatures spoil your plans.

of the leading ride manufacturers of the era, it is characterized by a 50-foot plunge and a unique roller coaster–style swooping drop.

Rhinefeld, now Germany, was located across a covered bridge from New France. With cobblestone streets, wrought iron, and stained glass adorning the buildings, it could fit right in the fatherland. The Wilcommenhouse restaurant served authentic German food and resembled an old town hall. It was adorned with a three-story Glockenspiel that chimed

Rhinefeld, one of the park's original themed areas, features the glockenspiel and Busch fountain. BUSCH GARDENS EUROPE

every fifteen minutes. In front, a courtyard was adorned with a fountain commissioned in 1914 by the wife of company founder Adolphus Busch following his death in 1913. It was brought to the park from St. Louis, Anheuser-Busch's hometown.

Rhinefeld also was home to the bulk of the park's rides. The largest was the Glissade, a 56-foot-tall, 2,862-foot-long steel roller coaster. It featured a unique spiral lift hill and a series of high-speed turns. The ride was designed by Anton Schwarzkopf of Germany, one of the most creative roller coaster designers of the time.

Although the Glissade represented the latest in amusement ride technology, the Kinder Karrousel represented one of the oldest. The Kinder Karrousel is an antique carousel originally carved in 1919 by the Allan Herschell Company. For much of its existence, the 55-foot-diameter, thirty-six-horse ride traveled the carnival circuit. It was eventually aban-

Glissade was Busch Gardens Europe's first roller coaster. DAVID HAHNER

doned in Dallas, Texas, where Anheuser-Busch located it in 1973. A team of fifteen craftsmen spent six months restoring it before placing it in its new home.

Rounding out the attractions in Rhinefeld was a fleet of 55-foot-long electrically powered river boats, which peacefully plied the 60-acre "Rhine River" that bisects the park, along with the Grimm's Hollow kiddie area.

Tying this diverse collection of areas together were a train and a sky ride. The train, with stops in Heatherdowns and New France, features two replicas of European locomotives that traveled along a 7,900-foot-long course. It crosses the Rhine River twice, including one trestle that measures 450 feet long and is 70 feet above the surface of the river. The sky ride is a one-of-a-kind creation. Rather than connecting two points like most sky rides, it is laid out in a 3,000-foot triangle joining Banbury Cross, Aquitane, and Rhinefeld.

By June 1975, everything was in place and the $30 million park opened to 8,000 enthusiastic guests. Word quickly spread about this one-of-a-kind place and by the end of the first season, nearly 1.6 million people had gone through the turnstiles, almost 20 percent above initial projections.

Growing Up

With such a successful debut, Anheuser-Busch knew that the park had to add more capacity, so a whole new land was created for the 1976 season. Dubbed Oktoberfest, in honor of the famous German fall festival, the new area occupied 10 acres next to Rhinefeld. In response to the long lines at the Wilkommenhouse, the heart of the new area was Das Festhaus, a 21,000-square-foot eating and entertainment facility. Billed as the largest festival hall outside Munich, Das Festhaus features a full menu of German food, live entertainment, and seating for 2,000 people.

But like its namesake in Germany, Busch Gardens' Oktoberfest is also known for its rides. Included that initial season were nine new rides, increasing the number at the park by 75 percent. In addition to spinning rides such as Der Wirbelwind, a swing ride; Der Blitzschneller, a trabant; and Die Schwarze Spinne, a spider ride; the area was home to a bumper car ride and Die Wildkatze. A steel roller coaster from Anton Schwarzkopf, it featured a compact 1,509-foot-long layout with a 44-foot drop. In addition, children were entertained by their own scaled down versions of the swings, bumper cars, airplanes, and a roller coaster.

As the 1970s was coming to a close, the theme park industry was locked in an all-out battle to build the tallest and fastest roller coaster. Not one to back down, Busch Gardens staked its claim in 1978 with the addition of the Loch Ness Monster, a roller coaster like no other.

The Festhaus was the anchor of the Oktoberfest themed area, which opened in 1976.

Taking advantage of the park's natural topography, the 130-foot-tall ride was built over the Rhine River with a 114-foot first drop pulling out just feet above the water at 60 miles per hour. Also nestled into the ravine were two interlocking vertical loops. In addition, the 3,240-foot-long ride features the

Monster's Lair, a spiraling turn of two and three-quarters revolutions in complete darkness. The bright yellow paint job created a stunning contrast to the thick trees, creating a spectacular icon for the park.

Opening a ride of this magnitude could not consist of a simple ribbon cutting. The Loch Ness Monster was christened with a flask of water from the real Loch Ness in Scotland. Also, the park invited some of the "Bravest and Meanest" people in the world including professional football players, race car drivers, a hockey player, and a mountain climber. Fortunately for them, they were able to conquer the beast.

Loch Ness Monster became an immediate landmark when it opened in 1978.
BUSCH GARDENS EUROPE

Leonardo's Garden of Inventions features several rides inspired by the inventions of Leonardo DaVinci. BUSCH GARDENS EUROPE

Loch Ness Monster became an immediate landmark and generated national publicity for the young facility with attendance surpassing 2 million for the first time. More room was needed for ever-increasing crowds. As a result, in 1980 it was decided to add a new country to the European tour with the development of Italy.

Located next to Banbury Cross, the $6 million area consisted of two sections. Near the Rhine River, where a brand new 300-foot-long bridge connected Italy to Oktoberfest, was an authentic Italian piazza featuring shops, an Italian restaurant, and a 1,000-seat outdoor theater, the Teatro San Marco. The area would be at home along the Mediterranean coast complete with porticos, covered walkways, stucco, brickwork, and red tile roofs. Observant visitors will even find ancient Roman graffiti.

Nearby was Leonardo's Garden of Invention, an immaculately landscaped formal Italian garden. It included two rides loosely based on the principals of science discovered by Leonardo de Vinci including the Battering Ram, a swinging boat ride; and the Flying Machine, a whirling contraption. Like the Loch Ness Monster, Italy was a huge hit with the guests leading to a 12.5 percent increase in attendance for the season.

Over the next couple of seasons, Busch Gardens focused on adding to Leonardo's Garden, installing DaVinci's Cradle, which takes riders in a 360-degree arc, and two kiddie rides including the one-of-a-kind Little Gliders.

Who's Afraid?

As 1984 dawned, unusual sounds were being heard from a corner of Rhineland. Although on the surface it seemed to be the growls of construction machinery, the noise was a little different. It sounded more wolflike. Busch Gardens was building a new roller coaster, and once again it would rock the roller coaster world. Throughout much of the off season, a 5-acre site was cleared, while Die Wildkatze was sold to make room for the new attraction. Unlike most roller coasters, the new ride featured cars that swung freely underneath the track. Built by Arrow Dynamics, the father of the Loch Ness Monster, the track is 2,800 feet long, with a maximum drop of 80 feet that makes a wide turn over the Rhine River at 48 miles per hour.

But the thrills did not stop with the ride structure itself. Riders travel in wolf-themed trains while howls permeate the air. Partway through the ride, the trains fly through an abandoned Bavarian Village, whose design was based on the German cities of Dinkelsbuhl and Rottenburg. Yes, The Big Bad Wolf had arrived at Busch Gardens. But with the opening of The Big Bad Wolf, Glissade seemed passé and gave its final rides at the end of the 1985 season.

Busch Gardens is about more than rides. Since it opened, the park presented a wide array of live entertainment that was updated every year. With so much attention being paid to the ride lineup during the first part of the 1980s, the park decided to break new ground with its shows in 1986.

The Big Bad Wolf is noted for its swooping turn over the Rhine River.

In Hastings, the Catapult ride was removed and an entirely new theater was created for the Enchanted Laboratory of Nostramos. The show
featured a one-of-a-kind combination of live actors, computer animation,
and special effects to tell the story of Northrup, a young alchemist appren-
tice. As the story unfolded, he takes wizardry into his own hands while
his master Nostramos the Magnificent is away. Northrup's tricks always
go wrong, resulting in a series of near disasters. Nostramos appears in a
magic mirror, and Northrup is shrunken to a height of 12 inches and
trapped inside a bottle. The Enchanted Laboratory soon became the most
popular show at Busch Gardens and by the time it ended its run in 2000,
31,000 shows had been performed in front of 5.5 million people.

Busch Gardens expanded on the other side of the park in 1987 with an
all new 4-acre area in Italy. Dubbed Festa Italia, the addition resembled an
Italian street carnival and with six rides themed to the journeys of Marco
Polo. Included were the Turkish Delight tea cup ride; the Chinese-themed
Sea Dragon spinning ride; Tradewinds, a circular ride honoring Polo's travels during the Crusades; and Elephant Run, an Indian-themed himalaya
for kids and their families. The largest attraction was the Gladiator's Gaunt-
let, a one-of-a-kind 46-foot-tall ride that was best described as an immense
taffy-pulling machine with seating for forty. Rounding out the section was a
relocated Catapult scrambler ride and a new station for the train ride.

Joining Festa Italia the following year was Roman Rapids in which
round six-person rafts travel down a 1,640-foot-long river past Roman
ruins, a spouting aqueduct, and other water hazards.

By the end of the 1980s, a new type of attraction was catching the attention of the theme park industry—the simulator, which transported riders
to another world using movie projection and motion simulation technology. One of the appeals of simulators were that parks could refresh them
every few years by changing the movie and special effects, essentially creating a new attraction. Busch Gardens jumped on the bandwagon with the
development of Questor. Located in Hastings, the 27,000-square-foot ride
took guests on a six-minute journey on the Questor. There they assisted
Alwyn, a mythical gnome, to search for a mystical crystal, encountering
several thrilling, often harrowing, obstacles along the way. At the heart of
the ride were two fifty-nine-seat, 35,000-pound ride simulation platforms
manufactured by Reflectone of Tampa, Florida, which also makes flight
simulators for the military.

A Dragon Roars

Menacing noises again arose from the woods of Oktoberfest in 1992 as
another steel monster graced the landscape. Busch Gardens returned to
Arrow for another groundbreaking roller coaster and it responded with

Drachen Fire represented the latest in roller coaster technology when it opened in 1992. BUSCH GARDENS EUROPE

Drachen Fire. With 3,550 feet of track, the 150-foot-tall ride featured a number of never attempted before elements. Included was a wraparound corkscrew inversion 120 feet above the ground as a prelude to a 140-foot drop; a camelback hump giving riders a zero gravity effect; a bat wing element with two inversions; an interlocking corkscrew; and a tight spiral.

Not only did the theme park grow in 1992, but so did Busch Entertainment's holdings in Williamsburg with the purchase of the nearby Water Country USA water park (see page 160).

Given the continuing success of the Enchanted Laboratory show, Busch Gardens decided to follow up Drachen Fire with another groundbreaking show. In 1993, the Globe Theatre was renovated into a 940-seat movie theater to accommodate Haunts of the Old Country, created by Busch Entertainment and Iwerks Entertainment, a leading creator of cutting-edge movies. Shot on location in England and Scotland, Haunts told the story of an eleven-year-old boy who stumbles across a friendly ghost while visiting a Scottish castle and gets a special tour. But this is not any old movie; in addition to 3-D imagery projected on a 30-by-60-foot screen, there was an array of special effects such as raindrops, fog, cold air, and flashes of light, making you a part of the action.

Since the park's recent expansion efforts had focused on older visitors, it was the park's youngest guests' turn to receive a new attraction in 1994. The old Grimm's Hollow kiddie area was transformed into the Land of the Dragons. This fanciful one and a half acre kid's attraction is the lair of Dumphrey the Dragon. Its centerpiece is a three-story-high, 30-foot-diameter tree house full of passageways, winding stairways, and slides. Surrounding the tree is a giant web of climbing structures, bridges, and play devices, including giant dragon eggs to climb through and fountains to splash in. There is a small theater and five dragon-themed kiddie rides

Land of the Dragons is a fanciful area for the park's smallest visitors.

including Eggery Deggery, a Ferris wheel with dragon egg cars, and Riffle Rapids, a miniflume with dragon-shaped boats.

While Land of the Dragons was introducing a whole new generation to the delights of Busch Gardens, construction was already under way on the park's next spectacular attraction. Between Banbury Cross and Leonardo's Garden of Inventions, 3-acre site was being cleared for another one-of-a-kind ride. Escape from Pompeii took a traditional amusement park splashwater ride and elevated it to a whole new level. Themed as an archeological dig, guests board boats for a tour of the ruins of Pompeii. After climbing

Escape from Pompeii takes guests on a tour of the famous ruins, ending with a splash. BUSCH GARDENS EUROPE

to the top of the attraction, the boats enter a large building to view the ruins; but things go wrong and the riders are menaced by earthquakes, fire, and falling structures. All of the sudden, the doors blow open and the boat plunges down a 50-foot hill for a drenching finish. As Busch Gardens' largest themed installation to that point, it became an immediate classic.

In 1996, the Anheuser-Busch Companies caught Olympic fever in honor of the Summer Olympics in Atlanta. Throughout the corporation, special promotions were under way and it was no different at Busch Gardens Europe where a special Olympic-themed ride debuted. Named Wild Izzy, after the games' mascot, it was a 45-foot-tall wild-mouse-style roller coaster from the German manufacturer Mack with a series of sharp turns along its 1,213 feet of track.

The roller coaster arms race was again raging in the late 1990s, and Busch Gardens jumped into the fray. Like the arms race in the 1970s, theme parks had an arsenal of new toys to compete with including the inverted roller coaster, a newly developed technology in which the cars traveled underneath the track, rather than on top of it. Combined with twisting drops and newly invented inversions the inverted roller coaster created a sensation of flying through the trees; it seemed to be a natural addition for Busch Gardens' unique terrain.

Ready for the 1997 season was Alpengeist. Located in Germany, the ride's name means "Ghost of the Alps" in German. The $20 million attraction is themed around an Alpine mountain region where an out-of-control ski lift snakes through the valley between Germany and New France. It was designed by Bolliger and Mabilliard, a Swiss firm that built its first ride in 1989. The firm soon established itself as the "Rolls Royce" of roller coaster designers with its smooth-riding, ground-breaking creations that became a favorite of roller coaster connoisseurs around the world.

Alpengeist was the tallest inverted roller coaster in the world when it opened in 1997.

Alpengeist opened as the tallest and fastest inverted roller coaster in the world, climbing to a height of 195 feet, with a first drop of 170 feet at 67 miles per hour. Its 3,828-foot-long track also featured six inversions including a vertical loop, a diving loop, a twin-inversion cobra roll, a heart-line spin, and a corkscrew. Like Busch Gardens' previous roller coaster installations, Alpengeist took the theme park industry by storm, yet again driving attendance to record levels.

An Event of Mythical Proportions

While Drachen Fire was groundbreaking when it opened, by the late 1990s, it was losing popularity in the face of newer attractions. As a result, it was closed in 1998, and Busch Gardens went looking for a replacement. With the success of Alpengeist, it was only natural to return to Bolliger and Mabilliard to design another roller coaster.

One of the other new types of roller coasters invented during the latest arms race was the hypercoaster, which forsook inversions in favor of large drops and high speeds. It was the perfect complement to the existing roller coasters at the park. The new ride would be the first hypercoaster that Bolliger and Mabilliard would create.

In spring 1999, Apollo's Chariot opened for visitors. The ride is based on Greco-Roman mythology, using the story of Apollo hauling the sun across the sky in his celestial horse-drawn chariot.

Replacing the Sea Dragon in Festa Italia, the towering ride lived up to its name, standing 170 feet tall, but taking advantage of the park's natural topography to create a 210-foot first drop over the James River at 73 miles per hour. That was followed by drops of 131, 144, and 102 feet along its 4,882 feet of track. In all, the ride's nine drops featured a total of 825 feet of vertical plunging, a world record.

The new attraction for the 2000 season—Jack Hanna's Wild Reserve— took on a completely different persona than Apollo's Chariot. Created in conjunction with the well-known wildlife advocate, the new attraction replaced the monorail station, which closed in 1998 and Threadneedle Faire, a Renaissance festival that was part of the Hastings area. The interactive area includes Eagle Ridge, a sanctuary for bald eagles that opened in 1993. Also featured is a display of American Grey Wolves set amid the ruins of a seventeenth-century castle and Lorikeet Glen, an aviary inhabited by lorikeets, small birds that will drink nectar from your hands and have no fear of landing upon your arms or head.

It had been two decades since a country had been added to Busch Gardens so it seemed like the time had come. For the 2001 season, Hastings was transformed into Ireland. The new 3-acre area provided an overview of the best of the Emerald Isle. Clustered around an Irish festival market, guests could enjoy strolling entertainment and attractions such as Irish Thunder, featuring Irish step dancers; the Secrets of Castle O'Sullivan, a special effects show; Grogan's, an authentic Irish pub and restaurant; and shops selling Irish products including Waterford crystal and Beleek china. In addition, King Arthur's Challenge, a simulator attraction that replaced Questor in 1996, was transformed into Corkscrew Hill, an all new 4-D simulator attraction that sends riders on a mythical Celtic journey through a land of giants.

The new area was christened by the mayor of Killarney, Ireland, and was so well received that attendance jumped by 17 percent, second only to the year the Loch Ness Monster opened. The new area's attention to detail was so accurate, it received an award from the Themed Entertainment Association, a trade group representing the "world's leading creators, developers, designers and producers of compelling places and experiences."

But that was not the only award received by what was by now recognized as one of the finest theme parks in the world; in 2002, Busch Gardens was presented with the Applause Award, the amusement industry's highest honor. Presented every two years, the international award recognizes a park whose "management, operations and creative accomplishments have inspired the industry with its foresight, originality and sound business development."

This originality was evident in 2003 when an all new 4-D movie debuted at the Globe Theatre, replacing Pirates 4-D, which opened in 1998. Busch Entertainment contracted with famous children's author R. L. Stine to create a story just for the attraction. The result was R. L. Stine's Haunted Lighthouse, a 25-minute 3-D film starring Michael McKean, Lea Thompson, and Christopher Lloyd, complemented by water sprays, misters, seat speakers, buzzers, and wind.

Two thousand and four was a relatively quiet year at Busch Gardens, with the primary focus on updates to its live entertainment lineup, including a new live animal show called Pet Shenanigans. In Oktoberfest, however, the Wild Maus—the renamed Wild Izzy—had scampered off to Busch Gardens Africa in Tampa. In its place, an ominous 40,000-square-feet building was beginning to take shape. For most of the season, just what would be in the building was a mystery; but once, an announcement was made, anticipation grew.

Cursed

By spring 2005, after three years of planning, design, and construction, Curse of DarKastle was ready. It is an attraction unlike any other ever built by Busch Entertainment. From the outside, it resembles an eerie fif-

Griffon features two vertical drops and a splashdown ending. BUSCH GARDENS EUROPE

teenth-century Bavarian castle, but inside, the ride represents some of the most cutting-edge amusement industry technology available, using 3-D projection, special effects, and motion simulation technology to take riders on a three-minute-and-twenty-second journey into ancient German folklore (see sidebar).

Although the 2006 season was highlighted by a new Emerald Beat show in Ireland and the return of Pirates 4-D in the Globe Theatre, Busch Gardens was again looking to the future. On July Fourth the LeMans car ride was retired to make way for another world-class roller coaster. Given the success of Alpengeist and Apollo's Chariot, the park again returned to Bolliger and Mabilliard to design its next steel monster—Griffon. "Like Nothing Else in the World," as the promotional billboards stated, the new 3,108-foot-long roller coaster sends riders up a 205-foot-tall hill, only to plunge down a 90-degree drop at more than 70 miles per hour. Riders also travel over a second 130-foot-tall vertical drop and through two Immelman loops, a simultaneous loop and roll named after a World War I German flying ace who invented the tactical maneuver. It ends with a splash through a pool. Adding to the thrill quotient are trains without floors, perching riders just a few feet above the tracks.

Busch Gardens Europe Today

In just three decades, Busch Gardens Europe has emerged as one of the world's finest theme parks, drawing praise from tourists, amusement park enthusiasts, and its peers in the industry. The park combines a stunningly beautiful setting, an immaculate attention to detail in its theming, and world class attractions using the latest available technology to create a theme park matched by few others. Today, the park features more than thirty rides and nearly a dozen live shows, along with a wide variety of other attractions including an animal area, artisans, and authentic shops.

Curse of DarKastle— a Don't Miss Attraction

Curse of DarKastle was one of the industry's most groundbreaking attractions when it opened in 2005. Not content with a traditional haunted house dark ride, Busch Entertainment decided to take things one step further and tell a story using the most cutting-edge technology available.

On the surface, guests approach DarKastle, a foreboding, ice-encrusted fifteenth-century Bavarian castle, and make their way through a landscaped courtyard. As they near the front portico and enter the building, blasts of cold air send a shiver up the spine. Now the story unfolds.

"Long ago in the deepest heart of the Black Forest, a young prince lived— unloved, neglected, in a dark castle." That prince is Ludwig, and as he grew older, his personality became darker. He developed a ruthless ambition that led him to take control of his parents' kingdom. Ludwig ruled with an iron fist and a cold heart and transformed his castle into a nightmare with secret passages and haunts to scare intruders. One day, he threw a lavish party, inviting those he believed were trying to usurp his power. The guests boarded golden sleighs for a tour and were never heard from again.

You are on that guest list and are led into the castle stables. After donning 3-D glasses, you board golden sleighs for a three-minute-and-twenty-second journey through the castle where you are pursued by the evil king. The sleighs plunge into a fireplace spinning into the abyss. Skeletal knights menace riders with their

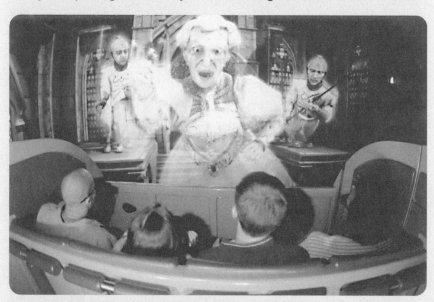

Curse of DarKastle immerses guests in the haunted castle of King Ludwig. BUSCH GARDENS EUROPE

weapons. A giant wolf swipes at riders and Ludwig's severed head appears to fly through the air. The ride ends with a steep plunge from the top of the castle.

At the heart of this attraction are the Golden Sleighs, actually eight-passenger ride simulators that move freely in all directions while traveling along a 1,000-foot-long track. The sleighs have high sides to focus vision forward on each of the eleven scenes, including nine in 3-D, that are projected on floor to ceiling screens. Combined with fire, ice, fog, and other special effects, the technology creates a completely immersive experience.

A project this complex could not be the work of a single entity. Peckham, Guyton, Albers, and Viets, of St. Louis, which created the original design for Busch Gardens Europe, served as the architect. Several companies from the theme park capital of Orlando, Florida, also played a role, including Falcon's Treehouse, the designer of the attraction; Nassal Company, which provided the theming; Oceaneering, which built the ride components; and Electrosonic, which developed the media and audio projection. For the actual movies, Busch Gardens went to Hollywood and hired the firm Super 78.

Parents need not be worried. Although the ride can be scary, the scenes are not gory and are cartoonish in nature. The park states that the Curse of DarKastle is appropriate for children as young as seven.

Guests enter the park in the England-themed area. The main attraction is the Globe Theatre, with its 4-D movies. Also found here are a number of souvenir shops, guest services, and the sky ride to France. Behind England is Scotland, originally known as Heatherdowns, home to the train ride to Festa Italia along with two of the park's most famous residents—the Loch Ness Monster roller coaster and the Budweiser Clydesdales.

A bridge transports guests to Ireland, home of the Corkscrew Hill simulator ride, along with authentic Irish shows like Emerald Beat, sh' and Grogan's Grille and Pub. From there, the park takes on a diff' personality as guests enter Jack Hanna's Wild Reserve where the experience Eagle Ridge, the Bald Eagle sanctuary; the America Wolf display; and Lorikeet Glen. The tour then returns to Euro with the appearance of France where the Griffon roller coaster donates the cafés and the sky ride station to Germany.

New France is next, a rustic trader's village where guests in enjoy leather, wood, and candle craftsmanship; live entertainme'; a train ride to Scotland; and the Le Scoot log flume. Another cov'ed bridge leads to Germany. In addition to the town center Glockespiel and a charming collection of shops, Germany is home to the Alpengeist inverted roller coaster, Kinder Karrousel antique carouse, Rhine River Cruise, and Land of the Dragons kiddie area.

Next door is the Oktoberfest where guests can enjoy authentic German food and entertainment at Das Festhaus, challenge the Curse of DarKastle, tame The Big Bad Wolf suspended roller coaster, or get spun silly on Die Wirbelwind, among others.

Another bridge crosses the Rhine River leading to Italy with its red tile–roofed buildings and ride-filled Leonardo's Garden of Inventions. Next door is Festa Italia, where several spinning rides and train transportation to New France are joined by the Roman Rapids water ride and Apollo's Chariot roller coaster. Connecting Italy to England is Escape from Pompeii, Busch Gardens' one-of-a-kind water ride.

WILLIAMSBURG

VIRGINIA

Water Country USA
OPENED 1984

Like its sister park, the understated entrance to Water Country USA is not in keeping with the delights that await within. What visitors find is a sprawling, lushly landscaped oasis filled with some of the best water attractions anywhere.

Looking around the operation today, it is hard to believe that it was not originally built by Busch Entertainment Corporation. Rather its history begins in 1982 when the 100-acre site was purchased by a group of nearly forty local investors. In mid-1983 construction started, and a mere 168 working days later, on June 14, 1984, Water Country USA opened for business. Built at a cost of $9 million, it was the first water park in Virginia.

That first season, the water park occupied 25 acres and featured five water attractions. Surfer's Bay was a huge wave pool to splash around in. Jet Scream consisted of four twisting waterslides, each 415 feet long. Rampage featured two 75-foot-long slides that riders plunged down on small sleds, skipping across water at the end. Runaway Rapids was a river ride, and kids could enjoy Polliwog Pond.

Water Country USA was well received by eager tourists and the fledgling facility expanded rapidly over the next several years. In 1987, the Lemon Drop and Peppermint Twist slides opened, both of which dropped riders into a pool after traveling through an enclosed tube. That was followed in 1989 by the Wild Thang, a waterslide featuring two-person rafts.

Water Country USA
176 Water Country Parkway
Williamsburg, Virginia 23187
800-343-794
www.watercountryusa.com

A New Era

By 1990, the facility had grown to encompass 40 acres with fourteen water rides, a pool area, and two live shows. Busch Entertainment Corporation saw that Water Country USA would make the perfect complement to its theme park and in 1992 reached an agreement to acquire it from the Rank Organisation. This large British conglomerate had purchased the park in 1990 from another British company, Mecca Leisure, which in turn purchased it in 1988 from its original owners.

Busch wasted no time in investing in the park to bring it up to their standards. Over the next several years, a major new attraction was an annual occurrence. In 1992, it opened Kids Kingdom, a new children's play area, followed in 1993 by the Malibu Pipeline, two enclosed tube slides of 468 and 318 feet, complete with strobe lights, water jets, a maximum drop of 55 feet, and an entrance and exit through a waterfall.

A second kid's area opened in 1994 in the form of Cow-A-Bunga, a 4,500-square-foot pool complete with waterslides, waterfalls, fountains, and water cannons, all overseen by the hilarious statue of a giant water-skiing cow.

Big Daddy Falls, a 670-foot-long waterslide accommodating four-person tubes that travel through two waterfalls, two cannon blasters, and a rain forest effect followed in 1995.

Water Country USA offers a damp diversion to guests of nearby Busch Gardens Europe. BUSCH GARDENS EUROPE

But Busch Entertainment was not done; H2O UFO, another water play area, opened in 1996, followed by the largest expansion in park history in 1997—Aquazoid. Aquazoid was not just any waterslide, but followed in the Busch Entertainment tradition of taking a standard theme park attraction to a whole new level. Billed as the world's largest special effects family raft ride, the attraction is based on a 1950s' mutant monster movie in which Aquazoid and Super Duck do battle as riders travel down a 78-foot-tall, 864-foot-long waterslide. As the rafts plunge into the tunnel, images of Super Duck chasing Aquazoid appear, highlighted by laser lights, fiber optics, and other special effects, while traveling through five water curtains before an underground finale.

Expansion continued in 1998 with the addition of Nitro Racer, a 320-foot-long, 52-foot-tall six-lane racing slide, followed in 2000 by Meltdown, Water Country's fastest and steepest water slide with an average speed of 22 feet per second along 701 feet of trough.

Most recently, Hubba Hubba Highway opened in 2003. A 1,500-foot-long river ride that covers 3 1/2 acres, the river adventure features a quick current and numerous action elements such as drenching coconuts, water jets, and geysers.

Water Country USA Today

From Virginia's first water park, Water Country USA has grown into the mid-Atlantic region's largest water park. With its 1950s and 1960s surf theme, the park features nearly two dozen waterslides, two river rides, a wave pool, three water play areas for kids, and even a live show.

The main entrance leads to a courtyard surrounded by changing facilities, a gift shop, and several food stands. Nearby are the Atomic Breakers, the Wild Thang, and the Rampage waterslides. The adjacent Caban-A-Rama Theater presents live shows. From there guests pass the Surfer's Bay wave pool; the Adventure Isle, home to Rambling River, and the Peppermint Twist and the Lemon Drop slides; and the Kritter Korral and the Cow-A-Bunga play areas.

Beyond Cow-A-Bunga are Water Country USA's largest attractions including Nitro Racer, Hubba Hubba Highway, Meltdown, and Aquazoid. The pathway then leads to the H2O UFO play area and the Big Daddy Falls, the Malibu Pipeline, and the Jet Scream slides.

Baja Amusements

OPENED 1981

THE COMMERCIAL STRIP KNOWN AS OCEAN GATEWAY, JUST WEST OF OCEAN City, Maryland, is not unlike similar areas throughout the country with its concentration of retail stores and fast food outlets. Ocean Gateway, however, has a rather unique feature distinguished by the roars of dozens of go-cart engines on a summer evening. The roar is coming from Baja Amusements.

Pursuing a Dream

The three Hoffman brothers, Steven, Brian, and James, were similar to many boys growing up in suburban American. With a fascination for all things mechanical, go-carts and minibikes were commonplace in their garage and driveway. As they grew up, Steven Hoffman got a job as a mechanic in the Washington, D.C., area, but he dreamed of operating his own business on the beach. One of his brothers owned a Honda Odyssey, a small dune buggy, and Steven thought that they could fill a summer renting dune buggies out to use at a track.

In 1981, the brothers journeyed to the resort community of Ocean City, Maryland, to try their luck and leased a 4-acre waterfront parcel. Its sandy soil was perfect to sculpt an elaborate dune buggy track that included 6-foot-tall banked turns. Despite a quality facility, however, the track saw minimal success initially as its location on a dead-end street severely restricted drop-in traffic, a critical component of any successful business in a resort area.

> **Baja Amusements**
> 12639 Ocean Gateway
> (U.S. Route 50)
> West Ocean City, MD 21842
> 410-213-BAJA (2252)
> www.bajaoc.com

As a result, in 1983, the brothers moved Baja Amusements a half mile away to a 4-acre site right on U.S. Route 50, the main artery into Ocean City. Although the new location had the advantage of being on a high-traffic route, the brothers used up all of their resources acquiring the parcel, meaning that funds for improvements were limited. Since the site was covered in trees, they had to focus their resources on clearing a track for the dune buggies. For much of that first season, the new facility had no utilities and improvements were made slowly as revenues came in.

But with the larger amount of traffic passing by, the new location proved to be much more successful than the older one. As a result, Baja Amusements was able to grow steadily over the next several seasons.

The Slick Track, which allows go-carts to slide through turns, opened in 1984. With plans to continue expanding, 6 additional acres were acquired in 1985, in part to accommodate the construction of the half-mile-long Road Racer track, still the park's largest. In 1986 the Family Track with its three leaf clover–shaped layout debuted along with a pond where riders could pilot miniature speedboats. A kiddie Speedway followed in 1987.

Reaching Its Potential

Through the 1980s business continued to grow and in 1989, Baja Amusements underwent a major expansion. The Honda Odyssey ride that started the business was removed and replaced with the Family Grand Prix track. The dirt that once formed the heart of the dune buggy track was relocated to the other end of the park to serve as the base for the new Safari Golf miniature golf course. A kiddie bumper boat ride was also added for younger visitors.

Opportunity presented itself in a different manner that year when Grand Cart went on the market. Located just a half mile west of Baja Amusements on Route 50, the park featured three go-cart tracks and a speedboat pond. Although it had fallen on hard times, the Hoffmans saw the complex as an excellent way to grow their business. They immediately launched an improvement program and succeeded in turning it around. Today, Grand Prix, as the park is now called, features eight go-cart tracks, bumper boats, and other activities on 10 acres.

Despite the attention that Grand Prix needed, Baja Amusements grew throughout the 1990s. The decade opened with the addition of a bumper boat ride in 1990, followed by the Rolling Thunder Raceway, a high-speed banked oval track with miniature stock cars, which replaced the speedboat ride in 1994. Then came the twisting Corkscrew track in 1995.

VISITING

LOCATION

Baja Amusements is located on U.S. Route 50, 1 mile west of the H. Kelly Memorial Bridge over Sinepuxent Bay and next to the White Marlin Mall.

OPERATING SCHEDULE

Baja Amusements is open weekends starting in March. Daily operations begin Easter weekend and continue through the first week of October, with weekend operations resuming until Thanksgiving. The park typically opens at 9 A.M. with closing time varying by time of year. During the peak summer season the park closes at midnight.

ADMISSION

Admission to Baja Amusements is free with attractions available on a pay-as-you-go basis ranging from around $1.50 for kiddie attractions to $10 for the Road Racer. Visitors can also purchase a wristband for around $35 that permits riders to use all rides and attractions for two hours.

FOOD

Baja Amusements' Snack Bar, located in the arcade building, offers hot dogs, pizza, and a full variety of snack items.

FOR CHILDREN

Baja Amusements offers a nice selection of rides for smaller children including the Wacky Worm roller coaster, the Frog Hopper, a merry-go-round, and the Rookie Track.

   Children under the age of eight ride free with an adult on the Family Grand Prix and the Family Track.

SPECIAL FEATURES

With eight tracks, Baja Amusements has one of the most diverse lineups of go-carts found anywhere. From the Rookie Track for beginners to the high-speed Road Racer and the Stock Cars, there is something to suit almost any taste.

TIME REQUIRED

Baja Amusements can be enjoyed in about two hours, although you might want to allow more time if you want to play miniature golf.

TOURING TIPS

Baja Amusements does the bulk of its business in the evening, so if you want to keep waiting to a minimum, visit in the morning or afternoon.

Baja Amusements features a diverse set of attractions.

Although Baja Amusements grew throughout the 1990s by adding larger go-cart tracks, there was little for smaller children to do other than the Rookie Track go-carts. For that reason, in 1998 the park added the Wacky Worm, a 13-foot-tall, 450-foot-long family roller coaster along with a merry-go-round. A Frog Hopper tower ride followed in 1999, the same year the go-cart lineup was rounded out with the addition of a high-speed Bullit track.

Baja Amusements Today

From a simple dirt dune buggy track, Baja Amusements has grown into a diversified amusement complex featuring eight go-cart tracks, bumper boats, a roller coaster, two kiddie rides, and a miniature golf course.

The main entrance to the park is home to the arcade, which is flanked by the Family Track and the Slick Track. Behind the arcade are the bumper boats, the roller coaster, the kiddie rides, and the Family Grand Prix track. Nearby are the Corkscrew and the Rolling Thunder tracks, with the Bullit, and Road Racer tracks next. Safari Golf is in the far corner of the park along Route 50.

Motor World

OPENED 1988

IT IS AN UNFORTUNATE SIDE EFFECT IN THE AMUSEMENT BUSINESS THAT in most instances when a major new amusement park is proposed, it fails to get beyond the planning stage, usually falling victim to funding shortages, zoning challenges, or shifting economic tides. Usually, those dreams quietly fade away, never to be heard from again. But in a rare instance, something does get left behind. Motor World in Virginia Beach, Virginia, is one such legacy.

Big Plans Deferred

Edward Garcia had long been a successful real estate developer in Virginia's Tidewater area. In the 1980s, he made plans to develop a multifaceted entertainment destination for the area. Not only was the area a popular tourist destination, but it had over a million year-round residents, creating a large potential market for a sizable attraction. He proposed a complex consisting of eight different entertainment venues each targeting a different segment of the marketplace. The facility would be named Ocean Breeze Festival Park. The two most elaborate areas were the Tivoli Experience, named after the famed Danish amusement park, and Old Virginia. The Tivoli Experience would feature nineteenth-century architecture, a lighted midway with mimes and face painters, a roller coaster, antique cars, and pedal boats. The colonial-themed Old Virginia would have horse-drawn carriages, a working gristmill, and colonial craftsmen such as blacksmiths, candle makers, and cabinetmakers. Other

Motor World
700 South Birdneck Road
Virginia Beach, Virginia 23451
757-422-6419
info@vbmotorworld.com
www.vbmotorworld.com

areas would be devoted to marine life, a water park, a go-cart park, an outdoor amphitheater, a miniature golf course, and sports activities.

For several years, Garcia and his company, ESG Development, worked to line up approvals needed to begin construction. Not only did they have to deal with the typical objections of local residents and businesses regarding noise and traffic, but also from nearby Oceana Naval Air Station, which was concerned about the impact that tall structures, including a proposed 140-foot-tall roller coaster, would have on the jets stationed at the base. But by 1984, the planning process had progressed to the point where the first phase, a water park, opened. Wild Water Rapids filled 20 acres with a large wave pool and several waterslides.

The next season marked the debut of the development's most recognizable landmark, Hugh Mongus. Originally sculpted in 1978 for a Richmond, Virginia, bank promotion, Hugh was a 65-foot-tall fiberglass gorilla that the park purchased and decked out in a swimsuit and sunglasses to beckon passersby into the complex. Although it was destroyed by an arsonist in 1989, allegedly by a flaming arrow to the abdomen, Hugh was rebuilt in 1996 by an Old Dominion University student as a graduate project, again making it a community landmark.

Motoring into Virginia

By 1988, ESG Development was ready to launch the next phase and developed a 27-acre parcel into Motor World. The entire complex carried a racing theme complete with car displays, go-cart tracks, and other

As its name implies, go-carts are the major attraction at Motor World.

VISITING

MOTOR WORLD

LOCATION

Motor World is located off Birdneck Road on the south side of Virginia Beach. From Interstate 264, take Exit 22 to Birdneck Road south for 3 miles. Motor World will be on your left about 1 mile past the golf course. From the oceanfront area, take Pacific Avenue south toward 1st Street. Go over Rudee Inlet Bridge and follow General Booth Boulevard one mile past the Virginia Aquarium. Look for Hugh Mongus, the 60-foot gorilla, and turn right.

OPERATING SCHEDULE

Motor World operates its paintball course, weather permitting, on weekends from 10 A.M. to dark during January and February. From March until late-May, the go-carts and miniature golf courses operate daily from 10 A.M. to dark, with the paintball course also operating on weekends. All of Motor World's activities operate from 10 A.M. to midnight between Memorial Day weekend and Labor Day. In September and October, the go-carts and miniature golf course open daily at 10 A.M., closing at dusk Sunday through Thursday and 10 P.M. Friday and Saturday. Go-carts, miniature golf, and paintball operate from 10 A.M. to dusk, weather permitting on weekends in November and December.

ADMISSION

Admission to Motor World is free. Visitors have the option of paying by the ride, with tickets costing between $4 and $6, or purchasing a multiride wristband. Wristband prices vary between $20 and $40 depending on the number of rides desired and the height of the rider.

FOOD

Motor World features one food stand offering pizza, hot dogs, sausage, and other sandwiches.

FOR CHILDREN

Kiddie City is the main kids' area offering a half dozen rides including the Motor World Express roller coaster. The dinosaur and elephant kiddie rides are located in the back of the park near three of the kiddie tracks.

Both the Grand Prix and the Family Tracks offer two-seat carts so children can ride along with an adult.

SPECIAL FEATURES

Motor World has one of the largest collections of go-cart tracks in the country with eleven circuits ranging from the Power Wheels track to the Speed Track.

The Speed Track and the Road Racer are two of the longest and fastest go-cart tracks in the country making them a must for carting enthusiasts.

(continued on page 170)

VISITING (continued from page 169)

MOTOR WORLD

TIME REQUIRED

To fully experience Motor World, plan on spending at least three hours. A quick sampling can be accomplished in about two hours.

TOURING TIPS

Visit during the afternoon to avoid crowds.

Combine a visit to Motor World with the neighboring Ocean Breeze Waterpark for a full day outing. Admission to Ocean Breeze is around $21, although discounted evening tickets are available.

motor-themed attractions. The main attractions were the five go-cart tracks, each with a distinctive target market. The Road Racer track, a quarter-mile twisting road track, was the largest, featuring cars imported from Lola of England with a top speed of 35 miles per hour. Other major tracks included the Speed Racers, the Family Track, and the Rookie Racer. Also featured was a large bumper boat ride. But what really made Motor World stand out from other similar facilities was the extensive variety of activities for children. Younger visitors had two scaled-down go-cart tracks in the form of the Mini-Moto cars and the Mini-Ferraris, along with the Souped Up Semis truck ride, the Micro-express train, kiddie bumper boats, and the Happy Haulers play area.

Motor World provided the perfect complement to Wild Water Rapids and when ESG opened a thirty-six-hole miniature golf course next to Motor World in 1989, it seemed that Ocean Breeze was well on its way to fulfilling its plans.

Unfortunately, fate intervened. Competition from the ever-growing Busch Gardens and Kings Dominion theme parks, along with a tougher financing climate in the late-1980s and early-1990s, pretty much ended ESG's plans to built Ocean Breeze Festival Park into a major destination. Only a batting cage complex was added after 1989.

But the halting of Ocean Breeze Festival Park's development did not mean Motor World stood still. By 1993, additional rides were added to Motor World including a mini-Himalaya spinning ride, a kiddie parachute tower, and kiddie elephant and dinosaur rides.

Motor World and the neighboring Wild Water Rapids water park continued to do strong business despite the change in development plans, but ESG Development found the complex increasingly outside its area of expertise. Although the 87-acre site did attract parties interested in redeveloping it for other uses, Edward Garcia sought to find another entertainment operator. "We still need a place for the kids and families to go," Edward Garcia told the local *Virginian-Pilot* newspaper. "The kids can't stay out in the hot sun all day." In 1996, the park almost reached a deal with Adventure Entertainment Corporation, which operated similar facilities in Florida, but unfortunately, it fell through.

A Change in Control

In 2000, it appeared that ESG had finally found a taker for Ocean Breeze's facilities. Wild Water Rapids was taken over by the Farrar family, which operated several water parks near Tampa, Florida. The family entered into a lease agreement with an option to purchase and launched a $1 million renovation of the 20-acre facility, which was renamed Ocean Breeze Waterpark.

Motor World was taken over by the Lazarus family, who got their start in the industry in 1976 when they opened Myrtle Beach Grand Prix in South Carolina. The success of that facility prompted them to open two more parks in the Myrtle Beach area in 1977 and 1990 that combined go-carts with kiddie rides and some water-oriented attractions to create a diversified entertainment complex. They were no strangers to Motor World, having worked with ESG Development on the facility's original design.

Motor World seemed to be the perfect fit for the family. The tourist-oriented economy of Virginia Beach resembled that of their home town of Myrtle Beach and the park, with its abundance of go-cart tracks and kiddie rides, was very similar to their South Carolina facilities. This meant that it would be very simple to bring it up to their standards with only cosmetic improvement and a new ride or two. "We're going to make some changes," Mark Lazarus told the *Virginian-Pilot* in January 2000.

But, as they say, one thing led to another and by the time the park opened for the 2000 season, the existing attractions were joined by a dozen new amusement park rides. Among the new additions were several rides from Chance Manufacturing of Wichita, Kansas, the largest manufacturer of spinning rides in the country, including a merry-go-round, the Sea Dragon swinging ship, and the Chaos and the Inverter, both of which spun and flipped riders in their own distinct way. Italian manufacturer Zamperla also provided some family rides including the Lolli Swing and Fire Chief, a "G-rated" version of the Inverter.

The main new attractions, however, were two new roller coasters. The Crazy Mouse was the larger of the two, standing 49 feet tall and featuring 1,377 feet of track highlighted by sharp turns that made riders feel like they would fall over the edge. Adding to the thrill element was specially designed cars that spun freely. For those that found the Crazy Mouse a little too intense, Motor World added the Wacky Worm, a 13-foot-tall, 444-foot-long family roller coaster from Fajume, another Italian manufacturer. Another attraction was a helicopter that offered tours of the area. "We want to be known as the amusement park of Virginia Beach," Mark Lazarus told the *Virginian-Pilot*. "We are diversifying to have more than just go-carts here."

The remaining undeveloped 40 acres of the original Ocean Breeze Festival Park were also put on the market and soon sold for development into an industrial park, killing Edward Garcia's dream once and for all.

Although the new strategy worked well initially, the economic downturn in 2001 disproportionately affected the tourism industry. As a result Motor World operators found themselves in bankruptcy and the new rides were removed. Motor World's future was again up in the air.

Although the 2000 expansion did not work out, the park's traditional go-cart-focused business remained solid. This caught the attention of Jim Loomis, owner of Midway Speedway, a go-cart and water park complex in Rehoboth Beach, Delaware, who stepped in during 2002. His launch of a major upgrade that season resulted in the addition of three new go-cart tracks—the twisting Grand Prix, the Super Eight Slick Track, and a kiddie track. In addition the former Slick Track was expanded into a new Outlaw track, and the Road Racer track was upgraded to accommodate more cars. The following year, the Sky Coaster, a 130-foot-tall swinging freefall attraction opened; and in 2004, the Road Racer track was upgraded with the first GTP Racing Karts in the world.

The Motor World Express kiddie coaster debuted in 2005.

In 2005, Motor World completed a major expansion of its kiddie offerings with the installation of Kiddie City, which featured four new kiddie rides to complement the existing himalaya, elephants, and dinosaurs. This included vintage classics such as the Midge-O-Racer car ride and the wet boats, along with the Motor World Express, a kiddie roller coaster originally built by the Allan Herschell Company.

The park moved in a new direction in November 2005 with the opening of VB Splat Zone, a large paintball course featuring two different fields of 37,500 and 15,000 square feet. A Junior Dune Buggy track followed in 2006, and in late 2007 the park's eleventh go-cart track, the Speed Track, featuring cars that can go up to 40 miles per hour, opened for business.

Motor World Today

Although the initial dreams for the original Ocean Breeze Festival Park fell by the wayside, they did leave behind two great attractions for Virginia Beach's residents and visitors. Motor World has grown into a unique amusement park featuring eleven go-cart tracks, including four for kids, kiddie and adult bumper boats, the Sky Coaster, and seven traditional kiddie rides. The park is laid out roughly in the shape of an oval. Taking the path to the right after entering the park, visitors come upon Kiddie City, home to most of the kiddie rides, the Road Racer Track, adult bumper boats, and the Sky Coaster. The Outlaw, Grand Prix, Speed, and Family tracks are all found in the back of the park. Next come three of the kids' tracks including the Kiddie, the Junior Stock, and the Junior Dune Buggy tracks. The Cannonball and Super Eight slick tracks fill out the oval.

Go-Karts Plus

OPENED 1989

ROBERT MILLER WAS WORKING IN A CORPORATE JOB WHERE, LIKE MANY people, his employer would transfer him to a new location every few years. In the late 1960s, he ended up in largely rural central Illinois. Although it had its charms, he soon realized, "I have nowhere to take my kids!" What soon transpired was the long process that resulted in Go-Karts Plus.

Sliding into the Business

Miller thought central Illinois was ripe for a small amusement park and started making plans to open one on Interstate 80, just outside the Quad Cities in Illinois, where a friend operated a campground. But fate intervened and he was transferred to Virginia Beach. Fortunately, the transfer did not derail his dream. In 1970, he quit his job and teamed up with a local lawyer and an architect to start making plans to open a theme park in Virginia Beach called Atlantis. A 55-acre site was acquired six blocks from the beach, and 500,000 ownership shares were sold at $10 each. As they worked through the financing, the partners decided to open a temporary amusement park to give them experience and provide a platform to promote Atlantis.

In 1974, Loop Amusement Park opened on a leased 2-acre parcel at the south end of the beach. Billed as "America's greatest small amusement park," the $1 million facility featured seven rides imported from Europe including a raceway, the UFO spinning ride, the Telecombat rocket ride, a merry-go-round, and the Glass House walk-through. Four of the rides

Go-Karts Plus

6910 Richmond Road
(U.S. Route 60 West)
Williamsburg, VA 23188

757-564-7600

www.gokartsplus.com

had never been seen in America before. All were to be relocated to the new park. The plan was to operate Loop Amusement Park for two years before opening Atlantis. But the oil crisis of the mid-1970s intervened, financing dried up, the small amusement park closed in 1975, and Miller's dream was again put on hold.

But Miller pressed on and took the rides to the resort of Myrtle Beach, South Carolina, where he set them up at Magic Harbor, a theme park that opened in 1968. At that time, the world's first commercial water-slide had just opened in town, and it was so popular that it was open 24 hours a day. This caught Miller's eye; it was just the opportunity he was looking for. He wanted to return to Virginia Beach, but someone was already building a slide there. His next thought was to go to the popular tourist destination of Williamsburg. "People told me I was nuts, I needed to be near the beach," he remembers.

Miller found a 4-acre site west of town and started construction. He had to haul in 5,000 truckloads of dirt to create a mound for the slide's cement trough, but it was worth the effort. Opened in 1977, it was one of the first waterslides in the country and business took off.

He followed up his successful debut in 1978 with a miniature golf course. Seeking to create the best facility possible, Miller hired a consultant from Myrtle Beach, which was known as a miniature golf mecca, to help him design a course for his fledgling business. He also studied hundreds of other miniature golf courses throughout the country to make sure it was the best one possible. Built for $178,000, one-tenth of what it would cost today, the new miniature golf course was highlighted by a waterfall and babbling brooks running through the facility.

Miller and his wife Ferne were hooked and in 1980, they opened a second golf course, Mini Golf America, in downtown Williamsburg.

A few years later, however, Miller sold the waterslide complex and moved to Orlando, Florida, where he opened another miniature golf course along the International Drive tourist strip. That turned out to be a fortuitous move, as the 1984 opening of Water Country USA in Williamsburg robbed so much business from the now antiquated slide that it soon closed and the complex was abandoned.

Now established in Orlando, Miller had been observing the success that his neighbor, a go-cart track, had been having and thought that would be a great way to expand his business. He heard about his original business sitting forlornly in the weeds and thought it was the ideal place to open a larger operation.

Miller sold the Orlando facility and returned to Williamsburg. At the time, family entertainment centers were starting to spread throughout the country. Essentially scaled-down amusement parks meant to capture time-pressed consumers for a couple of hours rather than an entire day, family entertainment centers typically offered up activities such as go-carts, arcades, and miniature golf.

The old waterslide was demolished and construction soon started on the new facility, called Go-Karts Plus. Miller had hoped to open in April 1989, but a constant stream of rain delayed construction and pushed the opening back to September 12. In addition to the original miniature golf course, which was upgraded, the park featured two go-cart tracks—the Figure Eight Track, with its over-under bridge, and the Euro Track, an oval-shaped "slick track" that allows the carts to slide around the corners. A bumper boat ride and a games arcade rounded out the offerings.

Go-Karts Plus was something different for the area, and soon became popular with visitors and residents alike. For 1990, a kiddie area was installed with a train ride and a play area.

In 1992, to help guide visitors to his new facility, Miller had a directional sign approved and erected at the closest Interstate highway exit. Although he met the state's strict requirements, the Virginia Highway Department later informed him that the attraction was not large enough to qualify for its own sign and ordered the sign's removal. Miller decided to fight the action and the classic "David versus Goliath" struggle caught the attention of the regional media. As a result, Miller got to meet with the state highway commissioner and went to the state legislature, which voted 95 to 1 against treating small businesses differently when it came to highway signage. In the end, Go-Karts Plus was the clear winner. The sign was re-erected and Go-Karts Plus received publicity conservatively valued by the park at $50,000.

Bumper boats were one of the original attractions featured at Go-Karts Plus.

LOCATION

Go-Karts Plus is located at 6910 Richmond Road (U.S. Route 60 West) in Williamsburg, Virginia, 3 miles off Exit 234 of Interstate 64. From the exit, take State Route 199 for 1¹/₂ miles to Lightfoot/U.S. Route 60 exit. At the end of the exit make a left onto U.S. Route 60/Richmond Road. Proceed through the next three traffic lights; the park is on the right after Williamsburg Pottery.

OPERATING SCHEDULE

Go-Karts Plus is open daily starting the last weekend in March at 5 P.M. weekdays and noon on weekends. Closing time is typically 9 P.M. From Memorial Day weekend through Labor Day, Go-Karts Plus is open 11 A.M. to 11 P.M. Hours vary in September and October, so call ahead.

ADMISSION

Admission to Go-Karts Plus is free with rides available on a pay-as-you-go basis. Tickets cost around $1.50 each with each ride taking between one and six tickets. Value packs offer a savings on the per ticket price.

FOOD

Go-Karts Plus has a snackbar offering hot dogs, ice cream, cotton candy, soft pretzels, and other snack items.

FOR CHILDREN

The park has three kiddie rides along with the Rookie Track and the Python Pit roller coaster. Kids three and under play free on the miniature golf course with a paying adult.

SPECIAL FEATURES

Go-Karts Plus has a wide variety of go-cart tracks ranging from the Rookie Track for kids to the high speed Stockarts.

TIME REQUIRED

Go-Karts Plus can be enjoyed in about two hours, although you might want to allow more time if you want to play miniature golf.

TOURING TIPS

During the summer, the park is least crowded between 3 P.M. and 6 P.M. and after 10 P.M.

  Discount coupons are available in many area tourist publications.

The Disk O was a major addition for Go-Karts Plus when it was installed in 2005.

Doubling the Fun

With the sign controversy behind them, the Millers could focus on building the business. Midway games were added, and in 1994 the park was able to purchase four adjoining acres, doubling its size. For the next two years, plans were made for the new acreage and in 1996, a $1 million expansion was launched. The main attraction was the Super Stockart Track, a high-banked oval track featuring vehicles resembling scaled-down race cars. Also added was a classic bumper car ride.

With the land almost full, expansion slowed for several years with only a couple of kiddie rides appearing.

In 2003, the Millers were attending the amusement industry's annual convention and a new ride from the Italian firm of Zamperla—unlike anything they had seen before—caught their eye. Called the Disk O, it consists of a 32-foot-tall U-shaped track. Along the track is a large disk seating twenty-four passengers that rocks, rolls, and spins riders as they face outward on a motorcycle-like seat. Noticing how enthusiastically the visitors to the show were reacting to it, the family assumed such a ride would cost nearly $1 million. When they discovered that the cost was only half that, they were sold.

In 2004, the Millers' hard work was recognized by the industry then they were presented with the Top FECs of the World award by the International Association of Amusement Parks and Attractions, which recognizes the industry's best-operated family entertainment centers.

The 2005 installation of the Disk O was followed in 2007 by a new family roller coaster, the Python Pit. An attraction that families with smaller children can enjoy, the 13-foot-tall, 300-foot-long ride was built by Miler Coaster. It originally operated at Jeepers! indoor kiddie parks in Cleveland, Ohio, and Gastonia, North Carolina, before being acquired by Go-Karts Plus.

The Python Pit replaced the existing kiddie go-cart track, which opened in 2002. A new, larger kiddie track, however, was erected next to Disk O and according to Miller, "Is the number one kiddie track in the world."

Go-Karts Plus Today

Robert Miller was a man with a dream, which has grown from a simple waterslide into Go-Karts Plus, a full-scale family entertainment center featuring four go-cart tracks, bumper boats, a roller coaster, two family rides, three kiddie rides, and a miniature golf course. The arcade serves as the front entrance to the facility. Leading up behind the arcade are the bumper boats, miniature golf course, kiddie rides, and the Figure Eight and Euro Tracks. To the right of the arcade are the Python Pit, the Disk O, the Rookie Track, the Super Stockart Track, and the Bumper Cars.

Virginia Beach Amusement Park

OPENED 2000

YOU CAN SEE IT FROM BLOCKS AWAY: A TOWERING CONTRAPTION RESEM-
bling a gigantic disembodied airplane propeller twirling continuously.
Naturally, you are inclined to see just what this curiosity is. That's just
what Virginia Beach Amusement Park hopes you will do.

Seizing an Opportunity

The Carriage Inn was typical of so many motels that opened in Virginia
Beach in the early 1960s. Featuring forty rooms a block away from the
beach and fishing pier, it was a favorite destination of vacationers for
decades. But by the 1990s, as the community was remaking itself, the
aging property fell out of favor to newer properties in the neighborhood.
Although there were no definite redevelopment plans, the owners
decided that the best strategy was to tear down the red brick structure
and convert it to a parking lot while they decided just what to do with
the prime parcel.

By late 1999, the vacant lot came under the control of food service
operator Bruce Mimran. Initially, he had no idea what to do with the
parcel, but it soon occurred to him that the town was lacking an amusement park. "Every resort area I know of has an
amusement park," he told the *Virginian Pilot*.

Mimran teamed up with Ken Young, owner of
the Norfolk Tides, a local minor league baseball
team, to develop the site. With only an acre to
work with, space was tight, but they managed to
make room for seven rides, including a merry-go-

**Virginia Beach
Amusement Park**

15th Street and
Atlantic Avenue
Virginia Beach, VA 23451
757-422-2307
www.virginiabeach
amusementpark.com

round acquired by the pair, and six other rides provided by Midwestern Midways, an Illinois company. Among the rides leased to the park were three spinning rides, the Himalaya, the Tilt-A-Whirl, and the Tornado, as well as a Spiral Slide; the Raiders, a walk-through attraction; and the Sky Wheel. The Sky Wheel was a rare Ferris wheel ride that featured two small wheels on either end of a long boom, which also rotated. Standing 87 feet high it provided a view several miles to the north and south along the beach and out into the Atlantic Ocean.

Virginia Beach Amusement Park opened on July 1, but it was soon evident that the joint venture between Mimran and Midwestern Midways was not working out. Mimran and Young claimed that the rides arrived at the site a month late and needed $20,000 in repairs to get them in working order. Midwestern Midways countered that they were not being paid their lease fees. By August, the case ended up being argued in the Virginia Supreme Court, which ruled that Midwestern Midways had the right to remove its rides from the park. With only the merry-go-round and a few games remaining, the new park ended its first season quietly. But Mimran and Young were not deterred, and sensing a renewed opportunity, quickly started to make plans to bring in a new set of rides to populate the site for the 2001 season.

Starting Over

Seeking to avoid the problems of the previous season, the partners decided to purchase the rides, rather than team up with a third party. In a way, it was good that the rides from the first season were removed as they were replaced by even more thrilling attractions. The centerpiece of the revived park was the Skyscraper, a 165-foot-long metal arm mounted on a base of four beams that seats two riders at each end. The arm spins like a propeller at speeds of up to 60 miles per hour.

Nearby, the park installed a log flume from French manufacturer Reverchon. The compact ride features eight log-shaped boats and packs two drops of 30 and 40 feet into just 750 feet of trough. Initially the ride ran into problems as it was erected too close to nearby power lines forcing the park to disassemble and rebuild it farther away.

Other attractions included the Super Loop in which a train traveled inside a large loop; the Hurricane, a spinning ride that dives up and down; a Music Express, originally manufactured in 1969 for Coney Island in New York and completely restored; the Dizzy Dragon spinning ride; the Hip Hop tower ride; and two kiddie rides, the train and the jets.

Unfortunately, the Super Loop did not live up to expectations and in 2003, it was replaced by the Cosmic Storm. Mimran developed the concept for the ride and worked with Stefano Moser, a third-generation

Like many seaside facilities, Virginia Beach Amusement Park offers a wide variety of rides packed into a small area.

builder of carnival rides from Verona, Italy. Although occupying only a small area, the Cosmic Storm packs in a lot of action by rotating at 16 rpms on four different axes, pulling maximum forces of 3 *g*s.

In 2004, the Inverter, another looping, flipping contraption opened at the park, replacing the Dizzy Dragon. With space at a premium, however, and Mimran's desire to keep the park fresh for repeat visitors, in 2006 the Inverter gave way to two classic spinning rides, the Tilt-A-Whirl and the Round Up.

Virginia Beach Amusement Park Today

With its abundance of flashy high-speed rides, it's hard to miss Virginia Beach Amusement Park along the thriving Atlantic Avenue tourist strip. Entering from the street, visitors find a tightly packed park with action in all directions. The Hurricane swoops and dives above patrons, soon followed by the flashing lights and loud music of the Music Express. Next comes the flipping, twisting, spinning Cosmic Storm, which is across the midway from the Big Splash log flume. The Skyscraper occupies a place of honor in the center of the rear portion of the park. It is surrounded by rides such as the Round Up, the Tilt-A-Whirl, the Hip Hop, and the kiddie rides.

 VISITING

LOCATION

Virginia Beach Amusement is located at 15th Street and Atlantic Avenue. From Interstate 264 East, which becomes 21st Street, go to Pacific Avenue. Turn right and go south to 15th Street. Turn right one block to Atlantic Avenue. Parking is available in neighborhood lots and street spaces, including the city-owned lot across Atlantic Avenue.

OPERATING SCHEDULE

The park is open mid-March through April on Friday evening from 5 to 11 P.M., and weekends from 1 to 11 P.M. Between May 1 and mid-June, the park is open daily, from 5 to 11 P.M. on weeknights and 1 to 11 P.M. weekends. From mid-June to Labor Day, operating hours are 1 to 11 P.M. daily. In September, the park is open weekday evenings from 5 to 11 P.M. and weekends 1 to 11 P.M. They are also open select days in October and November weather permitting. Please call ahead.

ADMISSION

Admission to the park is free. Ride tickets cost $1 each with rides taking between four and six tickets. A pay-one-price is available for around $20 during the afternoon and around $30 for an all day pass from 1 to 11 P.M. The Skyscraper costs an additional $20.

FOOD

The park features four food stands serving a variety of snack items including pizza, hot dogs, burgers, ice cream, and cotton candy. The nearby Atlantic Avenue tourist strip also contains a wide variety of food options.

FOR CHILDREN

Although the park only features two kiddie rides, several of the other attractions including the log flume and the Hip Hop tower can be enjoyed by most members of the family.

SPECIAL FEATURES

The Skyscraper is a must for thrill seekers as the 165-foot-tall attraction provides an intense ride along with a spectacular view of the surrounding neighborhood.

TIME REQUIRED

Virginia Beach Amusement Park can be enjoyed in about two hours.

TOURING TIPS

With its location in the heart of the Virginia Beach tourist district, a visit to the amusement park can be combined with a trip to the beach and the other attractions in the neighborhood for a full day's outing.

Blue Diamond Amusement Park

OPENED 2004

IT'S NOT UNCOMMON FOR AMUSEMENT PARK DEVELOPERS TO TEAM UP the rides and games with other complementary attractions. At several parks, lodging facilities are offered to allow visitors to extend their stay. Others have zoos, beaches, recreational activities, and even nature preserves. But there is only one place where you can combine an amusement park visit with a motocross race, Blue Diamond Park in Delaware.

A Unique Development

Greggo and Ferrara, a long-established construction contractor based in New Castle, Delaware, had a dilemma. The company owned a 400-acre parcel at a prime location near the convergence of three highways just south of Wilmington. It was underutilized with part of it being used as a quarry and the remainder sitting vacant.

The owners, however, sensed an opportunity. In Delaware, all-terrain vehicles and unlicensed motorcycles are not allowed on public property. Furthermore, there was no motocross racing track in the state, and only one BMX track. They thought that this need could serve as the basis for a diversified entertainment complex that could potentially occupy 200 acres with sports-oriented activities including a sports arena, a paintball field, an in-line skating rink, and a driving range. In 1998, plans were launched to bring the concept to reality.

By 2002, after almost four years of planning, construction was underway on two tracks. One

**Blue Diamond
Amusement Park**
765 Hamburg Road
New Castle, DE 19720
302-832-2999
information@bluediamond
park.com
www.bluediamondpark.com

was a 1.4-mile motocross track designed by Gary Bailey, a nationally known professional motocross rider and instructor; the other was a 38-acre combination all-terrain vehicle (ATV) riding area and state of the art BMX track built by American Bicycle Association engineers as an ABA-sanctioned course. The 85-acre complex opened in late August 2003 at a cost of $7 million.

Although plans were being made for the next step, development of the complex took a fateful turn in late 2003 when the company heard about a large steel roller coaster that was being sold by DelGrosso's Amusement Park in Tipton, Pennsylvania, to make room for new attractions. The prospect of opening Delaware's first major roller coaster since Shellpot Park in Wilmington closed in 1933 held great appeal. As a result, the concept of Blue Diamond Park was expanded to include an amusement park anchored by the DelGrosso's roller coaster.

A deal was soon reached to purchase the ride for $110,000 and Blue Diamond Park sent a Pennsylvania amusement ride company, Jim Houghton Enterprises, to DelGrosso's to dismantle the ride and ship it to Delaware. The crew arrived at the park, deep in the mountains of central Pennsylvania in January. They found the roller coaster buried under 18 inches of snow and another 6 inches of ice that had to be removed before work could begin. The crew, however, managed to get the ride taken down and placed on sixteen tractor trailers for the journey to its new home where a fifteen-member crew refurbished the coaster, painting it and adding new electrical wiring.

The purchase of the Blue Diamond Streak roller coaster marked the facility's transition into a full-blown amusement park.

Miniature golf is one of Blue Diamond Park's most popular activities.

At 55 feet tall and 1,710 feet long, it is one of the largest rides produced by Italian roller coaster manufacturer Pinfari. It is also one of the industry's most well-traveled rides. The coaster was originally installed in the early 1970s at Adventureland, Addison, Illinois, and was known as the Super Italian Bobs. When that park closed in 1977, the ride was relocated to Legend City in Tempe, Arizona, where it was renamed the Sidewinder. Legend City closed in 1983 and the roller coaster was again on the road, this time to South Dakota where it was the featured attraction at Wild West World, a newly developed amusement park in Custer. Unfortunately, that park closed in 1986 after only three years of operation and the coaster was acquired by DelGrosso's Amusement Park.

The owners knew that the new amusement park could not consist of just the roller coaster, renamed the Blue Diamond Streak. As a result, construction was started on two miniature golf courses landscaped with 5,000 shrubs and plants and a waterfall cascading over a wall of rocks. Also added were more than a dozen other amusement park rides including a merry-go-round, a Tilt-A-Whirl, a Scrambler, a giant slide, a custom-built swing ride, acquired from Pacific Park, Santa Monica, California; the Orient Express, a kiddie roller coaster; and several other kiddie rides. In addition, the Sky Diver, a Ferris wheel–type attraction that allowed riders to rotate the cars, was erected at the highest point in the park to make Blue Diamond's presence known to passing motorists.

LOCATION

Blue Diamond Amusement Park is located south of Wilmington, Delaware. From Interstate 95 take exit 4A (Christiana Mall exit) to State Route 1 South for approximately 4 miles. Exit off of State Route 1 to the left at 156B (North Wilmington). Merge on to U.S. Route 13 North. Turn right at first traffic light. Blue Diamond Park's entrance is on the left.

OPERATING SCHEDULE

Blue Diamond Amusement Park's season begins on Memorial Day weekend and is open from 11 A.M. to 9 P.M. on Wednesdays, Thursdays, and Sundays and 11 A.M. to 10 P.M. on Fridays and Saturdays. Regular operations end on Labor Day, although the park is in operation the first two weekends of September.

ADMISSION

Visitors to Blue Diamond Amusement Park have two admission options. They can pay a gate admission for around $4 and purchase individual tickets, which cost about $2 for kiddie rides, $3 for adult rides, and $4 for the Blue Diamond Express roller coaster. Visitors also have the option of purchasing an all-day pass for under $20, which provides gate admission and unlimited access to the rides.

FOOD

The park features three food stands. The main stand is the Blue Diamond Grille, which serves burgers, hot dogs, chicken fingers, ice cream, and popcorn. Other stands offer snack items including funnel cakes and lemonade.

FOR CHILDREN

Blue Diamond Park's six kiddie rides are clustered together to the left of the main entrance. Other family rides include the Orient Express roller coaster, the double-deck merry-go-round, the Tilt-A-Whirl, the Scrambler, and a slide.

SPECIAL FEATURES

The Blue Diamond Express roller coaster is one of the largest "portable" roller coasters ever built.

The park features a number of classic spinning rides that are rare in today's amusement parks. These include the Sky Diver, the Loop-O-Plane, the Paratrooper, the Spider and the Fish kiddie ride.

The Intruder is a one-of-a-kind attraction. Riders are seated in a circle, each with their own electronic "cannon." As the ride spins and climbs, a robot rises out of the center and riders score points by shooting it with their cannon.

TIME REQUIRED

To completely experience Blue Diamond Amusement Park, plan to allot at least three hours, more if you plan to take in a race at one of the tracks or play minia-

(continued on page 188)

VISITING (continued from page 187)

ture golf. If you are pressed for time, the major attractions can be enjoyed in less than two hours.

TOURING TIPS

Visit during the afternoon as crowds tend to be lighter.

Check out the facility's racing schedule beforehand and combine a visit to the amusement park with a race at the Motocross, the BMX, or the R/C (remote control) Racing tracks.

Unfortunately, rainy weather resulted in Blue Diamond Amusement Park's opening being delayed from Memorial Day weekend until July 4, 2004. To make matters worse, the rainy spring was followed by additional bad weather from Hurricanes Bonnie, Charley, and Gaston.

Getting Bigger and Better

The owners were undaunted by the challenging first season and launched a major improvement program for 2005. A new management team was brought in and a number of rides were removed to make way for ten new rides.

A double-deck merry-go-round was purchased from a mall in New Jersey to be the park's centerpiece. Also acquired were a Spring Tower ride from Cliff's Amusement Park, Albuquerque, New Mexico; a vintage Loop-O-Plane from Gillian's Wonderland Pier, Ocean City, New Jersey; and three rides from the recently shuttered Miracle Strip Amusement

Blue Diamond Amusement Park features a wide array of spinning rides.

Park, Panama City, Florida. These included the Matterhorn, a high-speed circular ride; the flipping Inverter; and the kiddie Enterprise. Other new attractions included a bumper car ride, a Tilt-A-Whirl, a Paratrooper, and two more kiddie rides.

The additions led to a much more promising 2005 season and expansion continued. The one-of-a-kind Intruder and the classic Paratrooper debuted in 2006. Two race courses for remote control vehicles joined the race tracks in 2007, and the amusement park saw the addition of five new rides. A Spider spinning ride and three kiddie rides were acquired but the major development was the acquisition of a second flagship ride, a log flume, to accompany the Blue Diamond Streak. Purchased from Steel Pier in Atlantic City, New Jersey, the ride was manufactured by Reverchon of France and features 750 feet of trough and drops of 30 and 40 feet.

Blue Diamond Amusement Park Today

In just a few seasons, the Blue Diamond Amusement Park has become one of the largest amusement parks in the area, featuring over twenty rides, including two roller coasters and six kiddie rides, along with two miniature golf courses.

The park's main entrance leads straight to the double-deck merry-go-round, which is the heart of the park. To the left are the miniature golf courses, the kiddie rides, the Paratrooper, and the Intruder. The midway to the right of the merry-go-round passes the log flume and the Orient Express kiddie coaster before leading to several of the bigger rides including the Blue Thunder Matterhorn, the Inverter, the swings, the Tilt-A-Whirl, the Scrambler, and the Sky Diver. The Blue Diamond Streak roller coaster dominates the back of the park, which is also home to the bumper cars, the Loop-O-Plane, and the giant slide.

Adventure Park USA

OPENED 2005

INTERSTATE 70 BETWEEN THE MARYLAND CITIES OF FREDERICK AND BAL-
timore is like so many highways in this densely populated region. Amid
the heavy traffic, the landscape is a mixture of rolling hills, forests, shopping centers, and even a minor league baseball stadium. Despite this
variety, the appearance of a roller coaster off to the side of the road still
takes motorists by surprise.

Building on Success

Larry Stottlemyer is one of those entrepreneurs who is always looking to
build on his past successes. After getting married in 1965, he worked in
the printing business. Every day he would drive by a miniature golf
course on which he played during his youth, growing more and more
restless with his routine job.

He finally decided that he had enough of working for someone else and
looked to the miniature golf course as a way out. That facility was not
available; in 1978, he decided to start looking for a site around Frederick to
build his own course. For two years, he worked to make it a reality. Preferred locations were lost to other bidders, and leases and financing fell
through; but Stottlemyer was undaunted and
finally obtained a $150,000 loan.

Adventure Park USA
113 West Baldwin Road
P.O. Box 362
New Market, MD 21774
301-865-6800
info@adventureparkusa.com
www.adventureparkusa.com

In 1980, he was able to purchase a 1.6-acre
parcel in Frederick to build his golf course, a franchised Putt-Putt operation. But even though the
course was now open, it was not smooth sailing.
Skyrocketing interest rates forced Stottlemyer to

file for bankruptcy in 1983. Although he struggled to restructure the finances for five years, he was still able to continue to improve the operation. New investors helped build batting cages, and a pizza delivery business was added to increase revenues.

By the late 1990s his operation was thriving. In addition to two miniature golf courses, the site packed in batting cages, a laser tag arcade, and a water wars game. He wanted to keep growing, however, and was simply out of room. He would have to move.

Again he started the whole process. Searching for a site, planning the new park, and working through the arduous process of obtaining financing took over five years to complete. As he did once before, however, he pulled all the pieces together and on June 14, 2005, Adventure Park USA opened for business in New Market, about 7 miles east of his original park, which he closed in 2003.

Built at a cost of $11.5 million, Adventure Park USA is a large family entertainment center featuring a diverse array of attractions. Initially 12 of the 17½ acres were developed, with the remainder being held in reserve for the eventual development of a water park. At the heart of Adventure Park USA is a 24,000-square-foot western-themed building. Inside are enough attractions to fill a rainy day, including a large arcade, a 3,500-square-foot laser tag arena, a climbing wall, a play area for the kids, an inflatable bounce, and a ropes course in which customers negotiate a series of obstacles 13 feet in the air.

Several other attractions were installed behind the building including a paintball arena, two miniature golf courses, a 3,500-square-foot bumper boat pond, and two go-cart tracks—Blazing Trails, a twisting family track, and the Speeding Bullet, characterized by its slick turns. Children can enjoy the merry-go-round and the spinning tea cup rides.

A Wildcat Attacks

Although it took until July to get all of the attractions open, the first season was a success. Stottlemyer settled in, content to run the business for the foreseeable future. In 2006, however, Williams Grove Amusement Park, located near Harrisburg, Pennsylvania, announced that it was not reopening and put several of its rides up for sale. One was the Wildcat, a 45-foot-tall, 1,500-foot-long, steel track roller coaster that spent its first three decades touring the eastern United States.

The ride was built by the legendary Anton Schwarzkopf and originally opened in 1976 at Busch Gardens Europe in Williamsburg, Virginia. In 1983, it was removed to make room for a bigger attraction and acquired by Morgan Hughes, a well-known ride broker and concessionaire. He leased the roller coaster to Playland, Rye, New York, from 1984 until

This aerial view shows the variety of activities at Adventure Park USA. ADVENTURE PARK USA

1991, and then moved it to the Steel Pier, Atlantic City, New Jersey, where it operated from 1994 until 1998. When the lease ran out there, Hughes stored the ride for a few years, and then set it up in 2001 at Williams Grove, which he had owned for a number of years.

The idea to purchase the Wildcat was actually that of Stottlemyer's son Erik. He presented the idea to his father, negotiated the purchase, put together the financing, and supervised its relocation.

The ride was quickly dismantled and the track and support structure laid out on an empty parcel in the back of the park where it was sand-blasted and painted. A new, modern control system was installed, and the cars were sent out to be refurbished and themed as 1960s' muscle cars, including a Chevy Camaro, a Plymouth Barracuda, a Mustang, and even a 1960s' police cruiser.

Although the park hoped to have the ride operating by the end of the 2006 season, the extensive work and zoning complications delayed the opening until spring 2007. Although the delay was disappointing, Adventure Park USA did receive some consolation when they were presented with the Top FECs of the World award by the International Association of Amusement Parks and Attractions, which recognizes the industry's best-operated family entertainment centers.

LOCATION

Adventure Park USA is located off Exit 62 (Monrovia/Hyattstown) of Interstate 70. From the exit, take State Route 75 South to the first intersection, West Baldwin Road, and turn right. Adventure Park USA will be approximately one-half mile down the road on the left.

OPERATING SCHEDULE

Adventure Park USA is open year-round, with the outdoor activities being open, weather permitting. Hours during the summer are 10 A.M. to 10 P.M. daily. Winter hours are 11 A.M. to 8 P.M. weekdays and 11 A.M. to 10 P.M. weekends.

ADMISSION

Admission to Adventure Park USA is free with attractions available on a pay-as-you-go basis. For a $1 fee, visitors can purchase a debit card–type pass that will be downloaded with credits which can be used on the rides, attractions and arcade games. Credits cost approximately $1 for 10, although they cost less on a per unit basis the more you buy. Arcade games cost anywhere from three to 30 credits, while the cost for attractions range from 15 to 170 credits.

FOOD

The Chuck Wagon Café, located in the main building offers a wide variety of food items including pizza, burgers, hot dogs, chicken nuggets, ice cream, pretzels, and other snack items.

FOR CHILDREN

Adventure Park features several kids-oriented attractions including the play area and the bounce in the main building and the merry-go-round and the tea cups outside. The miniature golf courses are family friendly, and children taller than 36 inches can ride along with an adult on the Blazing Trails family go-cart track.

SPECIAL FEATURES

The Wildcat is a classic family-oriented roller coaster designed by Anton Schwarzkopf, one of the greatest designers of steel roller coasters.

TIME REQUIRED

With its free admission and pay-as-you-go price policy, Adventure Park USA can provide as much entertainment as your schedule permits. To give yourself time to sample the highlights, allow for two hours.

TOURING TIPS

The large main building is open year-round and offers enough activities to fill an afternoon no matter what the weather.

Adventure Park USA Today

If history is any guide, Adventure Park USA is definitely a facility with a bright future that will see continued growth for many years to come. Greeting visitors is the large western-themed main building that serves as the heart of the operation. Open year-round, it is home to a large games arcade, a laser tag area, an inflatable bounce, a ropes course, a kids' play area, and the Chuck Wagon Café. Exiting out the back of the main building, visitors are greeted by the two large, elaborate miniature golf courses. To the left is the paintball area. Heading to the right, visitors come across the merry-go-round, the tea cup ride, and the Wildcat roller coaster. Next comes the bumper boat ride, and the two go-cart tracks anchor the back of the park.

Other Amusement Facilities

- *Central Park Funland,* 1351 Central Park Boulevard, Fredericksburg, Virginia 22401. Indoor/outdoor entertainment center featuring two go-cart tracks, bumper boats, three other rides, laser tag, batting cages, and miniature golf. 540-785-6700. www.centralparkfun-land.com.

- *Chesapeake Beach Water Park,* 4079 Creekside Road, P.O. Box 400, Chesapeake Beach, Maryland 20732. Features eight waterslides, primarily for smaller children, a lazy river, and kids' activity pool. 410-257-1404. www.chesapeake-beach.md.us/majorattractions_waterpark.htm.

- *Family Recreation Park,* 21036 National Pike (U.S. Route 40), Boonsboro, Maryland 21713. Family entertainment center featuring three go-cart tracks, two kiddie rides, batting cages, miniature golf course, and a driving range. 301-733-2333. www.famrecpark.com.

- *Frontier Town Waterpark,* Route 611, Ocean City, Maryland 21842. Water park with family activity pool, lazy river, twin flume tower slide, and body flume. Adjacent miniature golf course. 412-641-0693. www.frontiertown.com.

- *Galewinds Amusement Park,* 3081 Chapman Road, Wytheville, Virginia 24382. Features four go-cart tracks and a miniature golf course. 276-228-3020.

- *Glen Echo Park,* 7300 MacArthur Boulevard, Glen Echo, Maryland 20812. Former amusement park converted into an arts center owned by the National Park Service. Many original buildings are still being used, and the park's antique carousel is still in operation. Other features include dancing in the original ballroom and facilities for a half-dozen arts organizations. 301-634-2222. www.glenechopark.org.

- *Grand Prix,* 12424 Ocean Gateway (U.S. Route 50), West Ocean City, Maryland 21842. Features seven go-cart tracks, bumper boats, play area, batting cages, and fun slide. 410-213-1278. www.grandprixoc.com.

- *Great Waves Waterpark at Cameron Run Regional Park,* 4001 Eisenhower Avenue, Alexandria, Virginia 22304. Water park with three waterslides, wave pool, and kids' activity pool. 703-960-0767. www. nvrpa.org/cameronrun.

- *Jungle Jim's Adventure World,* 8 Country Club Road, Rehoboth Beach, Delaware 19971. Water park with six waterslides, water coaster, lazy river, activity pool, and kiddie pool. Park also features five go-cart tracks, bumper boats, and miniature golf. 302-227-8444. www.funat junglejims.com.

- *Midway Speedway and White Water Mountain Water Park,* Highway One at Midway, P.O. Box 1066, Rehoboth Beach, Delaware 19971. Features five go-cart tracks, bumper boats, and miniature golf. Water park with three waterslides and a kiddie pool. 302-645-8064. www. rehobothfunpark.com.

- *Ocean Breeze Waterpark,* 849 General Booth Boulevard, Virginia Beach, Virginia 23451. Large water park with sixteen waterslides, wave pool, water play area, and kids' pool. 757-422-4444. www.ocean breezewaterpark.com.

- *Planet Fun,* Beltway Plaza Mall, 6000 Greenbelt Road, Greenbelt, Maryland 20770. Indoor amusement park featuring six rides, kiddie play area, and an arcade. 301-982-2444. www.planetfun.net.

- *Refuge Golf and Bumper Boats,* 6528 Maddox Boulevard, Chincoteague, Virginia 23336. Features go-carts, bumper boats, kiddie rides, and miniature golf. 757-336-5420. www.refugegolfandbumperboats.com.

- *65th Street Slide and Ride,* 211 64th Street, Ocean City, Maryland 21842. Features three waterslides, paddleboats, miniature golf, and batting cages. 410-524-5270. www.slidenride.com.

- *Smiley's Fun Zone,* 75 Fort Drive, McHenry, Maryland 21541. Features two go-cart tracks, bumper boats, miniature golf, and playground. 301-387-0059. www.smileysfunzone.com.

- *Thunder Valley Go-Kart Track,* 6531 Hidden Woods Drive, Roanoke, Virginia 24018. Features go-cart track, laser tag, miniature golf, play area, and arcade. 540-387-9477.

- *Viking Golf Amusements and Thunder Lagoon Water Park,* Coastal Highway at Lighthouse Road, Fenwick Island, Delaware 19944. Features go-cart track, miniature golf course, and water park with six slides, a kiddie pool, and an activity pool. 302-539-1644 (golf and go-carts). 302-539-4027 (water park). www.vikinggolfamusements.com.
- *Watkins Regional Park,* 301 Watkins Park Drive, Upper Marlboro, Maryland 20774. Large county park featuring antique carousel, miniature train, miniature golf, Old Maryland Farm, and nature center. 301-218-6700. www.pgparks.com/places/parks/watkins.html.
- *Wheaton Regional Park,* 2000 Shorefield Road, Wheaton, Maryland 20902. Large county park featuring antique carousel, miniature train, miniature golf, horseback riding, public gardens, and nature center. 301-495-2595. www.mcparkandplanning.org/parks/facilities/regional_parks/wheaton/index.shtm.

INDEX OF MAJOR RIDES IN OPERATION

in Virginia, Maryland, and Delaware

Roller Coasters

WOOD TRACK

Grizzly, Kings Dominion, opened 1982.
Hurler, Kings Dominion, opened 1994.
Rebel Yell, Kings Dominion, opened 1975.
Scooby's Ghoster Coaster, Kings Dominion, opened 1974.
Roar, Six Flags America, opened 1998.
Wild One, Six Flags America, opened 1986.

STEEL TRACK

Wildcat, Adventure Park USA, opened 2007.
Wacky Worm, Baja Amusements, opened 1998.
Blue Diamond Express, Blue Diamond Amusement Park, opened 2004.
Orient Express, Blue Diamond Amusement Park, opened 2004.
Alpengeist, Busch Gardens Europe, opened 1997.
Apollo's Chariot, Busch Gardens Europe, opened 1999.
Big Bad Wolf, Busch Gardens Europe, opened 1984.
Griffon, Busch Gardens Europe, opened 2007.
Loch Ness Monster, Busch Gardens Europe, opened 1978.
Python Pit, Go-Karts Plus, opened 2007.
Racing Coaster, Jolly Roger Amusement Park, opened 2007.
Wacky Worm, Jolly Roger Amusement Park, opened 2002.
Looping Star, Jolly Roger at the Pier, opened 1996.
Anaconda, Kings Dominion, opened 1991.
Avalanche, Kings Dominion, opened 1988.

Dominator, Kings Dominion, opened 2008.
Flight of Fear, Kings Dominion, opened 1996.
Italian Job Turbo Coaster, Kings Dominion, opened 2006.
Ricochet, Kings Dominion, opened 2002.
Shockwave, Kings Dominion, opened 1986.
Taxi Jam, Kings Dominion, opened 1997.
Volcano, The Blast Coaster, Kings Dominion, opened 1998.
Motor World Express, Motor World, opened 2005.
Haunted Roller Coaster, Planet Fun, opened 1996.
Batwing, Six Flags America, opened 2001.
Great Chase, Six Flags America, opened 1999.
Joker's Jinx, Six Flags America, opened 1999.
Mind Eraser, Six Flags America, opened 1995.
Superman—Ride of Steel, Six Flags America, opened 2000.
Two Face: The Flip Side, Six Flags America, opened 1999.
Tidal Wave, Trimper's Rides and Amusements, opened 1986.
Toboggan, Trimper's Rides and Amusements, opened 1969.
Wacky Worm, Trimper's Rides and Amusements, opened 2006.

Wooden Carousels

Note: In addition to the great wooden carousels operating at the amusement parks in Virginia, Maryland, and Delaware, the region has a number of classic wooden carousels operating at municipal parks and similar
facilities. For a complete listing, please visit the website of the National
Carousel Association at www.nca-usa.org. Wooden carousels at amusement parks include the following:

Busch Gardens Europe, manufactured in 1919 by the Allan Herschell
    Company, installed 1975.
Funland (McHenry, Maryland), manufactured in 1951 or 1952 by the
    Allan Herschell Company, installed 1994.
Trimper's Rides and Amusements, manufactured in 1902 by Herschell-
    Spillman, installed 1902.
Paramount's Kings Dominion, manufactured in 1917 by the Philadel-
    phia Toboggan Company, installed 1975.
Watkins Regional Park (Upper Marlboro, Maryland), manufactured in
    1905 by Dentzel, installed 1972.
Wheaton Regional Park (Wheaton, Maryland), manufactured between
    1910 and 1915 by Herschell-Spillman, installed 1982.

Dark Rides

Curse of DarKastle, Busch Gardens Europe, opened 2005.

Haunted Mansion, Funland, opened 1980.

Morbid Manor II, Jolly Roger at the Pier, opened 2006.

Nightmare Manor, Jolly Roger Amusement Park, opened 1998.

Scooby Doo and the Haunted Mansion, Kings Dominion, opened 2004.

Haunted House, Trimper's Rides and Amusements, opened 1962, expanded 1988.

Pirate Adventure Dark Ride (freestanding attraction), Atlantic Avenue, Virginia Beach, Virginia, opened 2000s.

Walk-Throughs and Fun Houses

Old Mine, Frontier Town, opened 1964.

Mirror Maze, Jolly Roger Amusement Park, opened 2005.

Treasure Cave, Kings Dominion, opened 1975.

Aladdin's Lamp Fun House, Trimper's Rides and Amusements, opened 1970s.

Mirror Maze, Trimper's Rides and Amusements, opened 1988.

Pirate's Cove, Trimper's Rides and Amusements, opened 1971.

Pirate Ship Fun House, Trimper's Rides and Amusements, opened 1999.

Log Flumes

Log Flume, Blue Diamond Amusement Park, opened 2007.

Le Scoot, Busch Gardens Europe, opened 1975.

Log Flume, Jolly Roger Amusement Park, opened 1983.

Skull Mountain, Six Flags America, opened 1997.

Shenandoah Log Flume, Kings Dominion, opened 1975.

Big Splash, Virginia Beach Amusement Park, opened 2001.

River Rapid Rides

Roman Rapids, Busch Gardens Europe, opened 1988.

White Water Canyon, Kings Dominion, opened 1983.

Renegade Rapids, Six Flags America, opened 1994.

BIBLIOGRAPHY

Books

Adams, Judith A. *The American Amusement Park Industry: A History of Technology and Thrills.* Boston: Twayne Publishers, 1991.

Anderson, Norman. *Ferris Wheels: An Illustrated History.* Bowling Green, OH: Bowling Green State University Popular Press, 1992.

Cartmell, Robert. *The Incredible Scream Machine: A History of the Roller Coaster.* Fairview Park, OH: Amusement Park Books; Bowling Green, OH: Bowling Green State University Popular Press, 1987.

Cook, Richard, and Deborah Lange. *Glen Echo Park: A Story of Survival.* Glen Echo, MD: Bethesda Communications Group, 2000.

Corddry, Mark. *City on the Sand: Ocean City, Maryland, and the People Who Built It.* Centreville, MD: Tidewater Publishers, 1991.

Crenson, Victoria. *Bay Shore Park: The Death and Life of an Amusement Park.* New York: W. H. Freeman and Company, 1995.

Denson, Charles. *Coney Island: Lost and Found.* Berkley, CA: Ten Speed Press, 2002.

DeVincent-Hayes, Nan, and John E. Jacob. *Images of America: Ocean City.* Vol. 1. Charleston, SC: Arcadia Publishing, 1999.

———. *Images of America: Ocean City.* Vol. 2. Charleston, SC: Arcadia Publishing, 1999.

DeVincent-Hayes, Nan, and Bo Bennett. *Rehoboth Beach in Vintage Postcards.* Charleston, SC: Arcadia Publishing, 2002.

Fried, Frederick. *A Pictorial History of the Carousel.* Vestal, NY: Vestal Press, 1964.

Griffin, Al. *Step Right Up Folks.* Chicago: Henry Regnery Company, 1974.

Kyrazi, Gary. *The Great American Amusement Parks.* Secaucus, New Jersey: Citadel Press, 1976.

Lawlor, Mark. *Brandywine Springs Amusement Park: Echoes of the Past, 1886–1923.* Newark, DE: M and M Publishing, 1991.

Mangels, William F. *The Outdoor Amusement Industry.* New York: Vantage Press, 1952.

Manns, William. *Painted Ponies: American Carousel Art.* Millwood, NY: Zon International Publishing, 1986.

O'Brien, Tim. *The Amusement Park Guide.* Old Saybrook, CT: Globe Pequot Press, 2003.

Reed, James. *Amusement Park Guidebook.* New Holland, PA: Reed Publishing, 1978, 1982, 1987.

Rhodes, Jason. *Images of America: Maryland's Amusement Parks.* Charleston, SC: Arcadia Publishing, 2005.

Woodring, Franklin P., and Suanne K. Woodring. *Images of America: Pen Mar.* Charleston, SC: Arcadia Publishing, 2005.

Magazines and Newspapers

ACE News. 1981 to present. American Coaster Enthusiasts, 1100-H Brandywine Boulevard, Zanesville, OH 43701-7303.

Amusement Business. 1961 to 2006. Billboard Music Group, P.O. Box 24970, Nashville, TN 37203.

Amusement Park Journal. 1979 to 1987. Amusement Park Journal, P.O. Box 478, Jefferson, Ohio 44047-0478.

Amusement Today. 1996 to present. Amusement Today, P.O. Box 5427, Arlington, Texas 76005-5427.

Carousel News and Trader. 1986 to present. Carousel News and Trader, 87 Park Avenue West, Suite 206, Mansfield, OH 44902-1657.

Inside Track. 1987 to 1997. Inside Track, P.O. Box 7956, Newark, Delaware, 19714-7956.

Merry-Go-Roundup. 1975 to present. National Carousel Association, 620 Park Ave., No. 167, Rochester, NY 14607.

NAPHA News. 1978 to present. National Amusement Park Historical Association, P.O. Box 871, Lombard, Illinois 60148-0871.

NAPHA NewsFLASH!!! 1993 to present. National Amusement Park Historical Association, P.O. Box 871, Lombard, Illinois 60148-0871.

Roller Coaster. 1978 to present. American Coaster Enthusiasts, 1100-H Brandywine Boulevard, Zanesville, Ohio 43701-7303.

Selections from 1908 *Street Railway Journal,* in *Traction Heritage* 9, no. 4 (July 1976), Indianapolis.

INDEX

ABOUT THE AUTHOR

JIM FUTRELL BECAME FASCINATED WITH THE AMUSEMENT PARK INDUSTRY at a young age as he followed the development of the Great America theme park near his boyhood home of Northbrook, Illinois. Since then, he has visited over 300 amusement parks around the world and ridden more than 400 different roller coasters. Through the years, Jim has worked as a consultant for several Pennsylvania amusement parks (Kennywood in West Mifflin, Idlewild in Ligonier, Conneaut Lake Park in Conneaut Lake Park, and Bushkill Park in Easton). He has authored numerous articles on the

industry, is an avid collector of amusement park memorabilia, serves as historian for the National Amusement Park Historical Association, and is on the Hall of Fame Committees of the International Association of Amusement Parks and Attractions. His first book, *Amusement Parks of Pennsylvania*, was released in 2002, followed by *Amusement Parks of New Jersey* in 2004, and *Amusement Parks of New York* in 2006. Jim lives with his wife Marlowe and three sons, Jimmy, Christopher, and Matthew, near Pittsburgh, where he works as a market research director for a regional economic development agency.